Contents

NATIONS OF THE WORLD

AUSTRALIA

Robert Darlington

www.raintreepublishers.co.uk
Visit our website to find out more information about Raintree books.

To order:
☎ Phone 44 (0) 1865 888113
📄 Send a fax to 44 (0) 1865 314091
💻 Visit the Raintree bookshop at www.raintreepublishers.co.uk to browse our catalogue and order online.

First published in Great Britain by Raintree, Halley Court, Jordan Hill, Oxford, OX2 8EJ, part of Harcourt Education Ltd.
Raintree is a registered trademark of Harcourt Education Ltd.

Produced for Raintree by the Brown Reference Group plc
Project Editor: Robert Anderson
Designer: Joan Curtis
Cartographers: Colin Woodman and William LeBihan
Picture Researcher: Brenda Clynch
Indexer: Kay Ollerenshaw

Raintree Publishers
Editors: Isabel Thomas and Kate Buckingham

Printed and bound in Singapore.

ISBN 1 844 21466 4 (hardback)
07 06 05 04 03
10 9 8 7 6 5 4 3 2 1

ISBN 1 844 21480 X (paperback)
07 06 05 04 03
10 9 8 7 6 5 4 3 2 1

British Library cataloguing in publication data
Darlington, Robert
    Australia – (Nations of the world)
    1. Human geography – Australia – Juvenile literature
    2. Australia – Geography – Juvenile literature
    I.Title
    919.4

A full catalogue is available for this book from the British Library.

Acknowledgements
Front cover: Aboriginal hunter
Title page: Sydney Opera House from the harbour with the city behind

The acknowledgements on page 128 form part of this copyright page.

Foreword

Since ancient times, people have gathered together in communities where they could share and trade resources and strive to build a safe and happy environment. Gradually, as populations grew and societies became more complex, communities expanded to become nations – groups of people who felt sufficiently bound by a common heritage to work together for a shared future.

Land has usually played an important role in defining a nation. People have a natural affection for the landscape in which they grew up. They are proud of its natural beauties – the mountains, rivers and forests – and of the towns and cities that flourish there. People are proud, too, of their nation's history – the shared struggles and achievements that have shaped the way they live today.

Religion, culture, race and lifestyle, too, have sometimes played a role in fostering a nation's identity. Often, though, a nation includes people of different races, beliefs and customs. Many may have come from distant countries. Nations have rarely been fixed, unchanging things, either territorially or racially. Throughout history, borders have changed, often under the pressure of war, and people have **migrated** across the globe in search of a new life or because they are fleeing from oppression or disaster. The world's nations are still changing today: some nations are breaking up and new nations are forming.

Australia is at once a very old and very new nation. Its **Aboriginal peoples** have occupied this great landmass for tens of thousands of years. They developed a way of life that was intimately tied to the extraordinary landscapes and wildlife they found about them and which, despite their diversity, drew them together. On the other hand, Australia has been a nation – in that word's usual, Western sense – for little more than 100 years. This second, immigrant nation largely grew by destroying the old Aboriginal 'nation'. One of the most pressing questions that faces all Australians today is how these two nations – old and new – can finally be reconciled and a genuine multicultural society achieved.

Introduction

AUSTRALIA

Australia is the largest island nation in the world. It covers a land area of some 7,692,000 square kilometres (2,970,000 square miles) – only slightly smaller than the USA – and is the smallest of the Earth's seven continents. It is located in the Southern Hemisphere, between the Pacific and Indian oceans.

Geographically, Australia is one of the most isolated nations on Earth, earning it at one time the nickname 'the Last of Lands'. To the north, across the Timor and Arafura seas, are Papua New Guinea and the island chains of Indonesia – Australia's nearest Asian neighbours – while hundreds of kilometres to the south-east are the islands of New Zealand. Australia's southern coast faces the vast ocean surrounding the frozen continent of Antarctica.

Travellers to inland Australia are struck by its sameness. It is the flattest and, after Antarctica, the driest continent. There are places where the landscape hardly changes for hundreds of kilometres. Yet Australia is a land of striking contrasts. It has busy modern cities, sleepy country towns and a vast, sparsely populated interior. Rugged mountains, dense forests, huge plains and remote deserts are all contained within its boundaries. Australia's isolation means that many of its rich native plants and animals are unique. Kangaroos and platypuses, for example, live nowhere else on Earth.

The kangaroo is one of Australia's most famous native animals. The baby kangaroo, or joey, spends several months in its mother's pouch after it is born.

FACT FILE

● Australia is 25 times bigger than Italy, yet Australia's population is about one-third that of the European country.

● Australia's name comes from the Latin word *australis*, which means 'south'. Before Europeans found Australia, maps included an imaginary southern continent called *Terra Australis Incognita* ('Unknown Southern Land').

● Australia has three time zones: Eastern Standard Time (EST), Central Standard Time (CST) and Western Standard Time (WST). CST is half an hour behind EST, while WST is two hours behind.

Australia has been inhabited for some 40,000 years. The earliest inhabitants and their descendants are called **Aborigines**, meaning '[the people] from the beginning'. For thousands of years, these hunter-gatherers wandered the continent, developing their own distinct culture. After 1788, the British founded several **colonies** in the continent, and the **colonists** set about imposing their own culture on the country and its first people.

By 1900, each of the British colonies controlled its own affairs. In 1901, Australia formed a federal government that linked the colonies. The new nation became known as the Commonwealth of Australia. Although it now had some political **independence**, it still had many legal and cultural ties with Britain.

Australia's flag and currency record the country's ties with the United Kingdom. The Union Jack appears in the upper left corner of the flag, while the Queen appears on bank bills. Other images, however, such as that of the bush poet 'Banjo' Paterson on the 10-dollar bill, allude to Australia's own distinctive culture.

ADMINISTRATION

Australia has a federal system of government and administration. This means that while the federal government is responsible for matters that concern the whole nation, the states and territories have responsibilities for education systems, courts, hospitals and many other matters. Local government provides a third layer of administration, with responsibilities that include the construction and maintenance of some roads and public housing.

The capital of Australia is Canberra, which is located in the Australian Capital Territory (ACT). Australia is a **constitutional monarchy** – that is, its head of state, or ruler, is the British monarch (king or

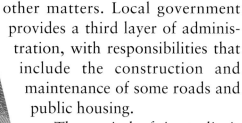

POPULATION DENSITY

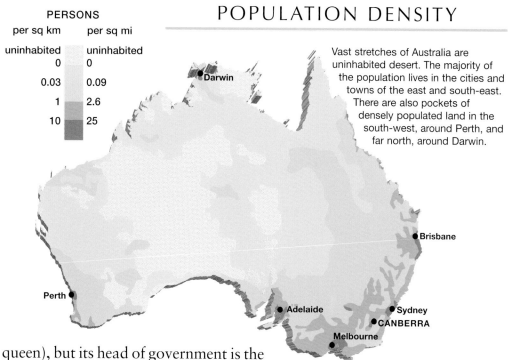

PERSONS

per sq km		per sq mi
uninhabited		uninhabited
0		0
0.03		0.09
1		2.6
10		25

Vast stretches of Australia are uninhabited desert. The majority of the population lives in the cities and towns of the east and south-east. There are also pockets of densely populated land in the south-west, around Perth, and far north, around Darwin.

queen), but its head of government is the Australian prime minister. Some Australians want to sever their country's relationship with Britain completely and make Australia a republic.

Australia's population has increased steadily over the last 100 years.

MONEY, FLAG AND SYMBOLS

The currency of Australia is the Australian dollar (A$). There are 100 cents to the dollar. Australia uses 5, 10, 20 and 50-cent coins, 1-dollar and 2-dollar coins and 5, 10, 20, 50 and 100-dollar notes. In the year 2001, the Australian dollar was worth about 40 pence.

When the Australian colonies became one nation in 1901, there was no Australian flag. The present design, although created in 1903, did not become official until 1953. Australia's flag represents its historic links with Britain. The British Union Jack sits at

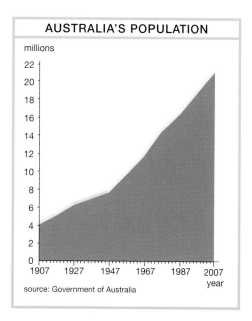

AUSTRALIA'S POPULATION

millions

source: Government of Australia

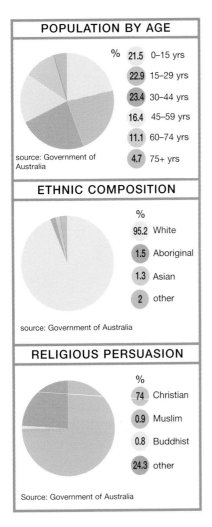

POPULATION BY AGE

%		
21.5	0–15 yrs
22.9	15–29 yrs
23.4	30–44 yrs
16.4	45–59 yrs
11.1	60–74 yrs
4.7	75+ yrs

source: Government of Australia

ETHNIC COMPOSITION

%	
95.2	White
1.5	Aboriginal
1.3	Asian
2	other

source: Government of Australia

RELIGIOUS PERSUASION

%	
74	Christian
0.9	Muslim
0.8	Buddhist
24.3	other

Source: Government of Australia

Australia's population is predominantly white, youthful and Christian. There are, however, important minorities of Asian and and Aboriginal people. The white population itself includes a variety of ethnic groups, including Greeks and Italians.

the upper left corner on a blue background. The stars on the flag represent the five stars of the Southern Cross, a constellation that can be seen clearly in the Australian night sky. The flag also features a large seven-pointed star representing the six states and the Northern Territory. If Australians choose to make their country a republic in the future, there may well be support for a new Australian flag.

Australia's **coat of arms** includes the emblems of the six Australian states. At the top is the seven-pointed star that appears on the flag. These are supported by two animals native to Australia, the kangaroo and the emu. Australia's unofficial national symbols are the wattle – a type of yellow-flowered acacia – and the eucalyptus.

LANGUAGE AND PEOPLE

Geographically, Australia is the world's sixth-largest country, but it has a comparatively small population of just under 19 million. This population is unevenly distributed across the continent. Most Australians live in a narrow strip of land along the eastern and southern coasts of the continent. Over 86 per cent of Australians live in cities and towns.

Today's Australians include people from almost every country in the world. They include the Aboriginal and Torres Strait Islander peoples, whose ancestors

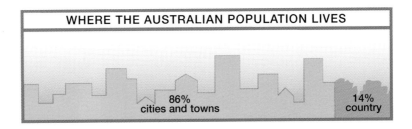

WHERE THE AUSTRALIAN POPULATION LIVES

86%
cities and towns

14%
country

have lived in Australia for at least 40,000 years, the descendants of the British and Irish settlers who colonized the country starting in the late 18th century and the millions of immigrants – mainly from Europe and Asia – who came to Australia in the last few decades of the 20th century.

English is the official language of Australia. However, the country is home to a variety of languages. More than five hundred languages and **dialects** were spoken by the Aboriginal peoples before the British arrived in 1788. Many of these languages are still spoken in parts of the country. English is spoken only as a second language by many people who came to Australia in the second half of the 20th century.

The Australian coat of arms includes two animals that are native to Australia, the kangaroo and the emu.

The national anthem

Until 1974, the British national anthem, 'God Save the Queen', was also the national anthem of Australia. In 1974, the federal government replaced it with 'Advance Australia Fair', which was written in 1878. The words of the anthem's first verse are:

Australians all, let us rejoice,
For we are young and free,
We've golden soil and wealth for toil,
Our home is girt by sea.
Our land abounds in nature's gifts
Of beauty rich and rare,
In history's page let every stage
Advance Australia Fair.
In joyful strains then let us sing
Advance Australia Fair.

Land and cities

'I was hardly prepared for this land of staggering contrasts, of unbelievable beasts, of the loveliest and strangest birds, of great modern English cities, of vast ranges that rivaled my beloved Arizona, and of endless ... bush.'

US author Zane Grey (1875–1939)

Australia is located in the Southern Hemisphere – that is, in the half of the Earth that is south of the Equator. When it is summer in the Southern Hemisphere, it is winter in the Northern Hemisphere, and when it is winter in the south, it is summer in the north. So, for example, when people in Europe and North America are wrapping up warmly to keep out the winter snow or winds in January, people in Australia are experiencing the hottest time of their year.

Australia is still largely a wilderness. The inland region is mostly the flat desert and uncleared country that Australians call the **bush**. Few people live in the bush; only the fertile coastal lands are densely settled.

Aboriginal peoples traditionally valued the land very highly and knew every natural feature in their own territory. Many landforms – for instance, a rocky outcrop or a distinctive hill – had religious importance for **Aborigines**. The geography of the land and its wealth were remembered from generation to generation in stories, songs and paintings.

Colonial Australians, too, were deeply aware of the wild landscapes that loomed beyond the settled regions. The **Outback,** as they called it, was a place of awesome beauty and power, not to be taken lightly. Even today, Australians are respectful of the vast, largely empty landscapes that dominate their country.

Uluru, also known as Ayers Rock, is the largest free-standing rock in the world. There are many Aboriginal myths and stories associated with it.

FACT FILE

- The Darling is Australia's longest river. It starts in the Great Dividing Range in eastern Australia and flows for more than 2740 km (1700 mi) to join the Murray River in the south.

- Because dry seasons (periods when there is little or no rainfall) can last up to eight months, about 30 per cent of Australia depends on artesian waters – underground waters reached by wells.

- Experts estimate that several Huon pine trees in south-west Tasmania are over 2000 years old, making them some of the oldest living things in the world.

Lake Mungo in New South Wales is today permanently dry. Thousands of years ago, however, Aborigines lived on the lake's plentiful fish, mussels and other wildlife. After Australia's climate changed some 20,000 years ago, the lake dried up.

ROCKY TERRAIN

The great continent of Australia was once part of the Antarctic landmass. Some 100 million years ago, the plate it sits on broke free and began floating northwards. Today, Australia is still drifting north towards Asia at the rate of about 50 millimetres (2 inches) per year.

Australia has been free of earthquakes, volcanoes and mountain-building forces for about 100 million years, longer than any other continent. This has allowed the wind and rainfall to wear the landscape down, so that today the dominant feature of Australia's landscape is its flatness.

Australia has some of the Earth's oldest known rocks. In Western Australia, there are rock crystals that scientists have dated back some 4300 million years. This means that the rocks were part of the Earth's original crust.

Sacred sites

Aborigines have a deep bond with the Australian landscape. They believe that before the arrival of humans in the land – a period known as the **Dreamtime** – spirits created all the landforms. The spirits could take on different forms, and, as they travelled through the unmade land, they left behind signs of their passing – a tree, hill or rock. Eventually, the spirits fell asleep, but their energy continued to flow through the land and through the people that lived there. For this reason, many natural sites are sacred to the Aborigines. Today, Aborigines sometimes protest when roads and dams are built on sacred land.

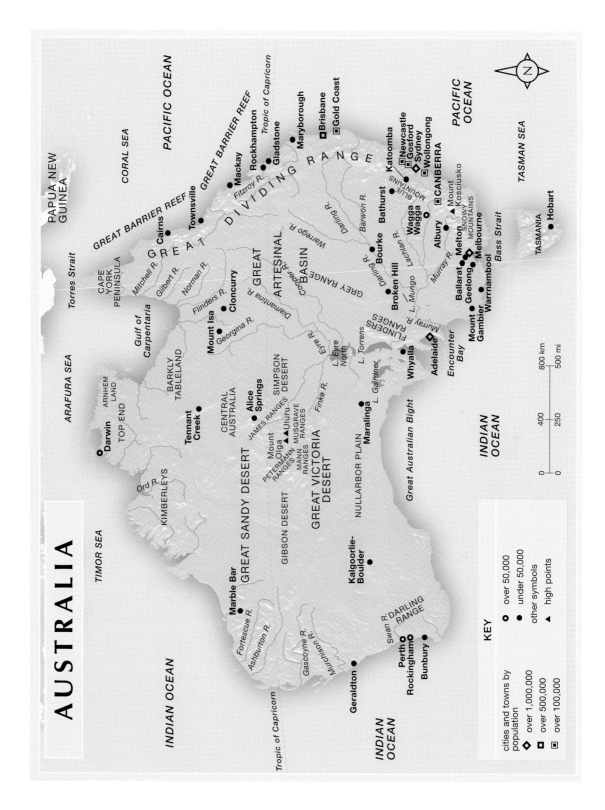

AUSTRALIA

PAPUA NEW GUINEA

PACIFIC OCEAN

CORAL SEA

GREAT BARRIER REEF

Tropic of Capricorn

Maryborough

■ Brisbane ▣ Gold Coast

Katoomba

▣ Newcastle
▣ Gosford
▣ Sydney
▣ Wollongong

Rockhampton
Gladstone

Mackay

Fitzroy R.

Townsville

Cairns

GREAT BARRIER REEF

Torres Strait

CAPE YORK PENINSULA

ARAFURA SEA

ARNHEM LAND

TOP END

Darwin

KIMBERLEYS

Ord R.

TIMOR SEA

Gulf of Carpentaria

Mitchell R.
Gilbert R.
Norman R.
Flinders R.

Cloncurry

Mount Isa

Georgina R.

Diamantina R.

BARKLY TABLELAND

CENTRAL AUSTRALIA

Tennant Creek

Alice Springs

JAMES RANGES

Mount Olga ▲ ▲ Uluru

PETERMANN RANGES
MANN RANGES
MUSGRAVE RANGES

GREAT SANDY DESERT

GIBSON DESERT

GREAT VICTORIA DESERT

SIMPSON DESERT

GREAT

ARTESINAL

BASIN

Cooper Cr.
Warrego R.
Barwon R.
Darling R.
Bulloo R.

GREY RANGE

Bourke

Broken Hill

Eyre Cr.

L. Eyre North

Finke R.

Maralinga

NULLARBOR PLAIN

Great Australian Bight

L. Torrens
L. Gairdner
L. Mungo

FLINDERS RANGES

Murray R.

Whyalla

Adelaide

Encounter Bay

Mount Gambier
Warrnambool

Geelong

Ballarat
Melton ▲ Melbourne

SNOWY MOUNTAINS
▲ Mount Kosciusko

Albury

Wagga Wagga

Bathurst

BLUE MOUNTAINS

CANBERRA ■

Lachlan R.

Murrumbidgee R.

D I V I D I N G   R A N G E

GREAT

Bass Strait

TASMANIA

● Hobart

TASMAN SEA

PACIFIC OCEAN

INDIAN OCEAN

Marble Bar

Fortescue R.
Ashburton R.
Gascoyne R.
Murchison R.

Geraldton

Swan R. DARLING RANGE

Perth
Rockingham
Bunbury

Kalgoorlie-Boulder

Tropic of Capricorn

INDIAN OCEAN

INDIAN OCEAN

KEY

cities and towns by population

◆ over 1,000,000
▣ over 500,000
▣ over 100,000

● over 50,000
● under 50,000

other symbols

▲ high points

0   400   800 km
0   250   500 mi

15

AUSTRALIA'S LANDFORMS

The central lowlands
These extend from the Gulf of Carpentaria in the north to Encounter Bay in the south. They include the Murray–Darling and Eyre Lake river systems. Apart from the Murray–Darling, most of the rivers are often dry.

The eastern highlands
Also known as the Great Dividing Range, these extend from Cape York Peninsula to the Bass Strait and include Tasmania.

The western plateau
This covers almost two-thirds of the Australian continent. It comprises three major deserts and a few low mountains at its fringes.

Place-names

Many of the place-names of Australia reflect the country's Aboriginal heritage. Such names come from the natural features of the landscape. For example, the port of Wollongong gets its name from the Aboriginal 'hard ground near the water'. Katoomba in the Blue Mountains, which is famous for its waterfalls, gets its name from *kedumba*, meaning 'shiny, falling water'. Other places in Australia are named after British towns or cities (Newcastle, for example) or British politicians (Melbourne and Sydney). Other names have stranger origins: an early governor of Sydney named Manly Cove after the 'manly' behaviour of the local Aborigines.

Outback and coast

The main geographical regions of Australia are the eastern highlands, the central lowlands and the western plateau. The central lowlands cover a vast area from the Gulf of Carpentaria in the north to Encounter Bay in the south. The monotony of this harsh landscape is broken only by salt lakes and rocky outcrops and a few low mountain ranges.

Few people live in this hot, dry area. Most of the population lives in the Murray–Darling Basin, where there is good grazing and wheat-growing land. Lake Eyre is the lowest point in the region – and on the Australian continent – lying sixteen metres (52 feet) below sea level.

On the east coast, bordering the Pacific, the eastern highlands are made up of a narrow fertile strip that merges with a continent-long chain of high plateaus and ridges called the Great Dividing Range. This is the remains of an ancient mountain range that once stretched from Cape York Peninsula in the north down to the Bass Strait in the south and across onto the island of Tasmania.

On average, the eastern highlands stretch 240 kilometres (150 miles) inland from the east coast. Most of Australia's population lives in this region, which has a warm climate, adequate rainfall and good farming land. Off the coast lies the system of **coral** reefs and atolls called the **Great Barrier Reef** (see pages 18–19).

The western plateau covers two-thirds of Australia and is mostly desert. On average, it is 300 metres (1000 feet) above sea level. In the north, desert runs right into the sea, but in the south, a strip of fertile land lies between low mountains and the Indian Ocean.

> The Great Dividing Range includes the highest summit in Australia, Mount Kosciusko – 2228 m (7310 ft).

Rare rivers

Australia has very few rivers and lakes. Many of the lakes in the interior are dry lakes that contain water only after heavy rain. Several inland rivers also have dry beds. After heavy rain, they can fill quickly, breaking their banks and flooding the plains for many kilometres around.

The only big river system is the Murray–Darling system. It drains an area of 1,072,000 square kilometres (414,000 square miles). Smaller rivers run from the highlands to the coast. These rivers are mainly in the south-eastern, eastern and northern parts of the country.

A river meanders through the flat landscape of the central lowlands. This river flows into Lake Buloke in southern Victoria.

17

The Great Barrier Reef

The Great Barrier Reef is a coral mass that stretches some 2000 km (1240 mi) along the Queensland coast, from the Torres Strait in the north to a spot roughly parallel with the port of Gladstone. At this southern end, the reef runs up to 300 km (180 mi) off the coastline, but in the north, it is much closer and sometimes broadens to a width of up to 80 km (50 mi).

Coral is created by small marine animals called polyps, which live huddled together. When the polyps die, they leave behind their 'skeletons', which form the rock-like material of the reef. New polyps grow on the reef – the rainbow of colours associated with coral comes from these living polyps. Since polyps need sunlight and warmth to grow, coral does not generally occur deeper than 30 m (100 ft) below the sea's surface. However, in places the coral grows at a depth of 60 m (200 ft).

Scientists are not certain how the coral first formed at this depth. One theory is that as the sea level slowly rose over thousands of years, the coral grew at a similar rate and was therefore always near the surface.

CORAL SEA

Cape
York
Peninsula

Cooks
Passage

Lark
Passage

Cooktown

Grafton
Passage

Cairns

Flinders
Passage

Townsville

Mackay

Swan
Reefs

QUEENSLAND

Rockhampton

Capricorn
Group

Gladstone

(Above) The Great Barrier Reef guards the Queensland coast, making sailing difficult. Breaks in the reefs provide ships with safe passages to the coast. (Right) The reef offers a brilliant display of brightly coloured fish and coral.

The Great Barrier Reef is the largest structure created by living organisms in the world. Most of the reef is about 2 million years old, but some areas are believed to be up to 18 million years old. Drilling on the reef has shown that the coral may be 500 m (1600 ft) thick.

The Great Barrier Reef is a rich natural habitat. Not only are there about 400 types of coral but also about 1500 species of fish, 4000 types of molluscs (clams and snails) and countless species of sponges, sea urchins, crabs and shrimps. Among the fish species that make their home on the reef are clown fish, butterfly fish and coral trout. There are also manta rays and whale sharks. The reef sharks are mostly harmless.

Dugongs – a type of sea-cow – humpback whales and many types of seabirds can also be found there. Six species of turtles lay their eggs on the sandy beaches of reef islands.

The crown-of-thorns starfish is a serious threat to the reef. It has eaten its way through large areas, destroying coral that has taken millions of years to grow. Other threats to the reef include pollution and tourism. Visitors to the reef must take care not to step on the fragile coral, or it will die.

With few natural barriers, such as mountains and rivers, Australia's states usually form 'blocks' of territory with straight, artificial borders.

THE STATES AND TERRITORIES

Australia is divided into six states and two territories. The six states are: New South Wales, Victoria, the island state of Tasmania, South Australia, Western Australia and Queensland. The territories are called the Northern Territory and the Australian Capital Territory, where the national capital, Canberra, is located. The federal government has more say over the affairs of the territories than it does over those of the states.

New South Wales

In 1770, Captain James Cook (1728–79) claimed all of eastern Australia for Great Britain. He called the land New South Wales. Because several new British **colonies** were begun in that area in the 19th century, the modern

STATES AND TERRITORIES OF AUSTRALIA

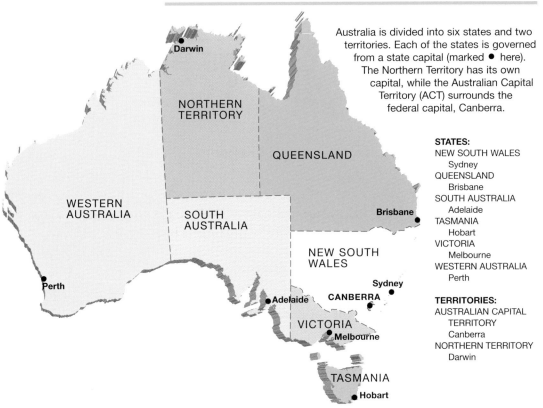

Australia is divided into six states and two territories. Each of the states is governed from a state capital (marked ● here). The Northern Territory has its own capital, while the Australian Capital Territory (ACT) surrounds the federal capital, Canberra.

STATES:
NEW SOUTH WALES
  Sydney
QUEENSLAND
  Brisbane
SOUTH AUSTRALIA
  Adelaide
TASMANIA
  Hobart
VICTORIA
  Melbourne
WESTERN AUSTRALIA
  Perth

TERRITORIES:
AUSTRALIAN CAPITAL
  TERRITORY
  Canberra
NORTHERN TERRITORY
  Darwin

state of New South Wales occupies just ten per cent of Australia. New South Wales is famous for its state capital, Sydney, and for its beautiful surf beaches. With 6.3 million people, New South Wales is the most populous state. Most of its people live in the cities of Sydney, Newcastle and Wollongong.

The region around these cities is the industrial heartland of the state. Two-thirds of Australia's coal is mined from deposits in the Hunter Valley, near Newcastle, and in the Illawarra region, around Wollongong. The Hunter Valley is also an important wine-making region.

Farmers grow a variety of crops in the fertile strip that stretches along the state's coast. Wheat is the most widely grown crop, and corn, potatoes, grapes, sugarcane and citrus fruits are also raised here. New South Wales also produces about half of Australia's timber. A major programme to replant trees has been organized by the government to ensure the survival of Australia's forests.

A short way inland, just beyond Sydney's western suburbs, lie the Blue Mountains, which are part of the Great Dividing Range. These mountains are not really blue. The millions of eucalpytus trees in the area release droplets of oil into the air. When light passes through these oil droplets, it makes the mountains appear blue from the plain below. The scenery in the mountains is spectacular, with sheer cliffs, waterfalls and dense forest.

To the south, the land rises to the Snowy Mountains. These mountains are the site of one of Australia's biggest hydro-electric projects, with sixteen large dams.

The Blue Mountains, west of Sydney, proved a formidable barrier to the early European settlers who wanted to explore the land to the west. It was not until 1813 that a successful attempt was made to cross them.

Saltbush is very common in arid areas of Australia. It gets its name because it tolerates salty soils. There are 302 species of saltbush in the country, including samphire and bluebush.

Further inland, the western slopes of the Great Dividing Range provide land for grazing sheep for fine wool. The western plains make up the remaining two-thirds of the state. Here, the country becomes flat, dry and thinly populated. Much of this area is part of the great Outback, with its red earth and plains of saltbush.

The main town in north-western New South Wales is Bourke, with a population of fewer than 3000 people. 'Back o' Bourke' is an old Australian phrase that refers to the town's position on the edge of the Outback. The only city in western New South Wales is Broken Hill. Its population of about 23,000 grew because of the silver, lead and zinc mining in the region.

Victoria: 'the garden state'

Victoria's Great Ocean Road has some spectacular sights. The Twelve Apostles are towering limestone pillars that stand some 65 m (215 ft) out at sea.

Victoria is the southern-most and the smallest of the mainland states. It is also the most heavily industrial-ized and has the most densely settled population. At 4.7 million, its population is second only to that of New South Wales. In the second half of the 19th century, Victoria's population far exceeded that of New South Wales. People were drawn to the region by its goldfields, which were the richest in the world at the time.

The rush for gold

In May 1851, E. H. Hargreaves found gold near Bathurst, New South Wales. The news prompted a rush of people to the area hoping to share in his good fortune. Workers deserted Sydney for the goldfields, and it seemed as if the workers of Melbourne would follow suit.

To stave off this disaster, the city's businessmen offered a reward for anyone who found gold within 300 km (190 mi) of Melbourne. Gold was discovered in the Yama River within a week, but a more promising discovery at Clunes inspired prospectors to head for central Victoria. In September, the biggest find yet occurred at Ballarat. By the end of the year, more than 250,000 ounces of gold had been claimed. Hopeful prospectors came from Europe, China and even from the exhausted goldfields of California. In 1852, about 1800 people were arriving in Melbourne every week.

The gold rush opened up lands previously known only to Aborigines and led to a period of phenomenal growth and prosperity for Victoria. Australia's population soared from 400,000 to more than 1 million in the first 12 years of the rush. Victoria's population alone grew from 77,000 to 540,000 in the same period.

Gold production decreased after the 1880s. However, by that time the population of Victoria was beginning to stabilize, and other activities such as agriculture began to take the place of gold mining in Victoria's economy.

Victorians call their state 'the garden state' because of its lush green landscape. The state does not have the extremes of temperature that can occur elsewhere in the country and gets more rainfall. Victoria's capital, Melbourne, is Australia's second-largest city. It is a major business centre and has some of the finest parks in the world (see page 49).

Central and western Victoria have historical gold-rush towns and fertile grazing lands. The north-east has high country rising to the ski slopes of Alpine and Mount Buffalo national parks. Gippsland in south-eastern Victoria has rich pastures and heavily wooded hills.

In the south, the Great Ocean Road runs for more than 300 kilometres (180 miles) along the coast and features some of the most spectacular scenery in Australia.

Tasmania gets its name from the Dutch navigator Abel Tasman, who landed on the island in 1642.

Tasmania: the island state

Unlike the other Australian states, Tasmania is an island. At 68,332 square kilometres (26,383 square miles), it is the smallest state. Tasmania also has the smallest population of any Australian state – fewer than half a million people.

While most of Australia is flat and dry, western Tasmania is one of the world's wettest and most mountainous places. Strong winds, called the 'roaring forties' – so called because they occur between 40 and 50 degrees latitude south – sweep across the ocean from below Africa and become loaded with moisture. When they reach the mountains of western Tasmania, the winds rise abruptly, drenching the region in rains and, occasionally, snow.

Heavy rainfall accounts for the beauty of western Tasmania. The south-west in particular is famous for its lakes, rainforests, waterfalls, fast-flowing rivers and the jewel-like colours of the mosses and lichen that cling to the rocks and trees.

The areas of greatest beauty in south-west Tasmania are all national parks. They contain rugged mountains, deep forests and alpine moorlands. This unspoilt wilderness has been listed by the United Nations (UN) as a World Heritage Site. The three big national parks in the area are Cradle Mountain–Lake St Clair National Park, the Franklin–Gordon Wild Rivers National Park and the Southwest National Park.

The Huon Pine

In a largely treeless continent, one of Tasmania's most valued resources has always been its forests. One of the world's sought-after timbers comes from a native Tasmanian tree, the Huon pine, which can be found only around the Huon River in the south-east part of the island. The tree is very slow-growing and long-lived – one specimen is thought to be over 2200 years old. Wood from the Huon pine is very strong. In the 19th century, it was valued as a timber for shipbuilding, and convicts laboured in some of the remotest forests in the world to harvest its timber. So popular was the wood that by the end of the 19th century, the Huon pine was an endangered species and the government had to limit its felling. Today, environmentalists and the timber industry continue to fight over the Huon pine.

People travelling from Tasmania's west into its north and east are struck by the contrasts in the countryside. The farmlands and small towns of much of the east are more like England than any other part of Australia.

Tasmania is called the 'Apple Isle' because it produces most of Australia's apple exports. It is also known as the 'Heritage Island' because many traces of its colonial past have been preserved.

Tasmania's population has not grown in decades because of the lack of economic growth. The Tasmanian economy is mainly agricultural, relying on farming and sheep and cattle grazing, though fishing, forestry and mining are also important. Hydro-electric power projects take advantage of the many fast-flowing rivers to produce cheap electricity for manufacturing. In the late 1990s, about one in four of the Tasmanian workforce was employed in manufacturing, mainly in food-processing industries.

Tasmania's capital, Hobart, is the second-oldest city in Australia. The heart of this old port is Constitution Dock, where numerous fishing boats are moored. In December, the dock is the destination of the famous Sydney to Hobart yacht race.

The Barossa Valley, north-east of Adelaide, is Australia's best-known wine-producing area. Many of the country's award-winning wines are grown here.

South Australia

South Australia is called the 'festival state'. This is because of its arts festival and the other cultural events that are held in and around its capital, Adelaide. Most of the state's 1.5 million people live in the capital. The most highly populated parts of South Australia are the coastal belt and the Lower Murray Basin.

Most South Australians are employed in manufacturing and service industries, while the most significant primary industries – those that use **natural resources** from the land – are mining, wheat-farming and wine-growing. Many experts say that the state produces some of the finest wines in the world.

Most of the state's 984,380 square kilometres (380,070 square miles) are desert. Eighty-three per cent of the state receives less than 250 millimetres (10 inches) of rain each year. The area around the Great Australian Bight has a Mediterranean climate, with cool, moist winters and hot, dry summers. Further north the land becomes hotter, drier and very thinly populated. This is one of the world's harshest and most remote areas. The land is normally dusty. Occasionally, however, a rainstorm floods the parched earth, transforming the land into a haven for bird life. Lake Eyre has filled with water just a few times since European settlers first came to South Australia in 1836.

To the north of the Salt Lakes region are the sand dunes of the forbidding Simpson Desert. Between the deserts and the Great Australian Bight lies the Nullarbor Plain, so called because nothing but saltbush grows on it – *nullus arbor* means 'no tree' in Latin.

The Simpson Desert has dunes of red sand that run in unbroken lines for more than 300 km (180 mi).

Western Australia

Western Australia occupies a third of the Australian continent. Yet, although it covers an area of more than 2,525,250 square kilometres (975,000 square miles), the state has a population of only 1.8 million.

Western Australia has a wide range of climates. The north has a monsoon climate, with a hot, wet season and a warm, dry season. The south-west has hot, dry summers and mild, wet winters. The most hospitable part of the state is a narrow strip of land along the south-west coast. This includes the state capital, Perth, where more than 60 per cent of the state's population lives.

Outback cafés such as this one in the Pilbara region of Western Australia are a welcome sight for travellers in arid and remote areas.

Most of the state is desert. The vast central area is made up of the Great Sandy, Gibson and Great Victoria deserts and is not suitable for any commercial land use. In the north, the Ord River Basin is now farmed widely thanks to an irrigation project that began in the 1960s.

The Kimberleys in the north are a rugged plateau used mainly for grazing beef cattle. The north-west is a huge dry area that receives most of its rain from **tropical** cyclones (storms) in late summer. The south-west is mainly a vast desert plateau covering most of the southern third of the state. More rain falls on its western and southern edges, allowing forests of giant karri and jarra trees to grow. Below the plateau and deserts, the Nullarbor Plain extends into South Australia.

Eighty per cent of Western Australians live in cities or in large towns. Much of the state's wealth has come from minerals. In the 1890s, there was a gold rush in the south-west. In the 1960s, the state had a second minerals boom based mainly on iron ore from the north-west. Few people work in mining, however, and most work in the manufacturing, trade, transportation and service industries.

The Bungle Bungles

Bungle Bungle National Park, also known as Purnululu, is a spectacular region in the Kimberley region of Western Australia. Covering 3000 sq km (1160 sq mi), the park is made up of deep, narrow gorges and strange-looking, beehive-shaped orange-and-black-striped rock towers. The orange stripes are formed by the mineral silica, while lichen makes the black ones. Until the early 1980s, much of this region was known only to the local Aboriginal people. The name *purnululu* means 'sandstone' in the local Kija **dialect**. 'Bungle bungle' is a mis-spelling of bundle bundle, a local grass.

The Northern Territory

With an area of 1,350,000 square kilometres (521,000 square miles), the Northern Territory is more than twice the size of Spain, but has a population of only 190,000. It has few paved roads, enormous distances between settlements, a harsh climate and a rugged, frontier culture.

The main industries of the region are mining, tourism and beef-cattle grazing. The first permanent European settlement in the Northern Territory was established in 1869. Aboriginal people, though, have lived there for about 40,000 years, longer than elsewhere in Australia.

The territory has two main regions – Central Australia and the Top End. Central Australia is about the size of France. It is blazing hot in the daytime but can be very cold at night. Most of the area is desert, and the droughts there can last for years.

Central Australia has a unique beauty that attracts visitors from all over the world. The dominant colour of the earth and rocks is a fiery red. The first Europeans to enter Central Australia called it the 'Dead Heart', but the region is far from dead. The desert has springs from underground water sources, and many plants thrive there. Central Australia is home to 172 permanent bird species, 70 species of reptiles – such as saltwater and freshwater crocodiles – and twenty species of mammals, such as the bilby, a rat-like creature that has rabbit-like ears.

Between October and December each year, the combination of intense heat and humidity in parts of the Northern Territory can affect some inhabitants' mental health. This condition is referred to locally as going 'troppo'.

This Aboriginal boy in Kakadu National Park, in the Northern Territory's Top End, is using a wooden spear to catch fish. There are about 50 species of freshwater fish in the billabongs (water holes) and rivers of the park.

Uluru and Kata Tjuta

Uluru attracts more visitors than any other place in Central Australia. It is the world's biggest free-standing rock formation, the surviving peak of a buried mountain range (see page 12). Uluru rises 348 m (1143 ft) above the surrounding plateau and is 9.4 km (5.8 mi) in circumference.

Uluru is one of about thirty similar dome-shaped rocks that rise from the desert plains north of the Musgrave Ranges. Collectively, they are known as the Olgas, or the Olga Rocks. Their Aboriginal name, *Kata Tjuta*, means 'many heads'. Mount Olga, the most westerly rock, is also the highest, at 460 m (1500 ft).

The Olgas lie within Uluru National Park, which is a United Nations World Heritage Site. These landforms appear to change their colours during the day.

The rocks are sacred to the local Aborigines. In 1985, the land in the park was returned to its Aboriginal owners, the Anangu people. It is now leased by them to the Commonwealth National Parks and Wildlife Service. Until that time, Uluru was called Ayers Rock. Today, however, the Aboriginal people prefer their name for the rock and park, Uluru, to be used. People need to ask to climb the rock (see also page 54).

The main town of Central Australia is Alice Springs, called simply 'The Alice' by its residents. Founded in 1890, it is now home to more than 27,000 inhabitants.

The only other significant town in the whole of Central Australia is Tennant Creek, 507 kilometres (315 miles) north of Alice. Most of the remaining population of Central Australia lives on huge cattle stations (farms) or on Aboriginal land.

About one in four people in Central Australia is Aboriginal. Until the 1970s, they lived on reserves (areas of land on which only Aborigines live), missions, cattle stations and on the fringes of country towns. Since that time, large areas have been transferred back to their traditional owners. Today, a third of all land in the territory is owned by Aborigines (see page 78).

The other main region of the Northern Territory is the Top End. It is tropical monsoon country – that is, it has wet and dry seasons rather than summer and winter. The capital of the Northern Territory, Darwin, receives almost all of its annual rainfall during the wet season, from December to April. Darwin has a population of about 78,000 people drawn from many ethnic backgrounds and is a bustling, modern city on an attractive harbour. On Christmas Day 1974, the city was almost destroyed by a cyclone (a fierce tropical storm; see box).

Large parts of the Top End are Aboriginal land. The largest of these areas is Arnhem Land. Kakadu National Park is owned by the Kakadju people, from whom it gets its name. It contains many of the

Top End climate and Cyclone Tracy

Because of its closeness to the Equator, the Top End experiences monsoons every year. These drenching rains begin at the start of each year and are sometimes accompanied by extraordinary lightning storms. For this reason, Darwin is the city most likely to be struck by lightning in the world.

Cyclones in the region occur most commonly at the beginning or at the end of the wet season. They can release 760 mm (30 in) of rain in 24 hours. Some cyclones exhaust themselves at sea, while others zigzag inland, causing chaos in their path.

Cyclone Tracy hit Darwin on Christmas Day 1974. At its peak, the winds were estimated to be blowing at 280 km/h (170 mph). Sixty-six people died in the disaster, and only 400 of Darwin's 11,200 buildings remained intact. The city's residents were evacuated, and many chose not to return.

New and rebuilt houses are now constructed with steel reinforcements so that they will be able to withstand cyclones.

The unusual-looking booyong tree grows in the rainforests of Queensland. Its root-like trunk can extend for many metres.

world's finest rock paintings, some of which are at least 23,000 years old. Kakadu has world heritage status both for these traces of ancient cultures and for its outstanding natural features. It includes swamps, shrubland, open forest and rainforest and has a huge variety of wildlife, including crocodiles.

Queensland: 'the sunshine state'

Queensland is Australia's second-largest state and is called the 'sunshine state'. At more than 1,727,000 square kilometres (667,000 square miles), Queensland is seven times the size of the UK. Most of its population of 3.4 million live east of the Great Dividing Range, mainly in coastal cities. These include Brisbane, the state capital, and the cities of Rockhampton, Townsville and Cairns.

Running parallel to the northerly part of the coast are the Great Barrier Reef islands. In the west is a high plateau with rich tropical forests. Queensland has many areas with good soils that produce sugar, cotton, peanuts and timber and provide fine grazing land for sheep and cattle. It is also rich in minerals. Its tropical climate makes it a popular tourist destination.

In the far north are Cape York Peninsula and the Gulf Country. The plains of the Gulf Country are very flat and are often flooded in the wet season (December to April). The central lowlands are hot, dry grass plains. In the mid-south of the state, the Darling Downs provide good land for sheep grazing and farming.

The Australian Capital Territory (ACT)

The ACT is a small area of just over 2400 square kilometres (930 square miles) in the south-east of New South Wales. It was created to provide land for the national capital, Canberra (see pages 42–44), where most of the region's 308,000 people live.

Australia's External Territories

In addition to its mainland territory and adjoining islands, Australia administers seven External Territories. All are tiny and remote island groups, of which only three are inhabited. Australia also claims about a third of the Antarctic landmass.

CORAL SEA ISLANDS

Northerly Coral Islands

Willis Island
Magdelaine Cays
Coringa Islets
Herald Cays
Tregrosse Islets

These uninhabited island chains lie in the Coral Sea to the east of the Great Barrier Reef. They officially became part of Australian territory in 1969.

Southerly Coral Islands

West Islet
Bird Islet
Cato Island

NORFOLK ISLAND

KINGSTON

English explorer James Cook discovered this lush island in 1774. Later, it became a British penal settlement. Today, it is home to some 2000 people, most of whom live in the capital, Kingston.

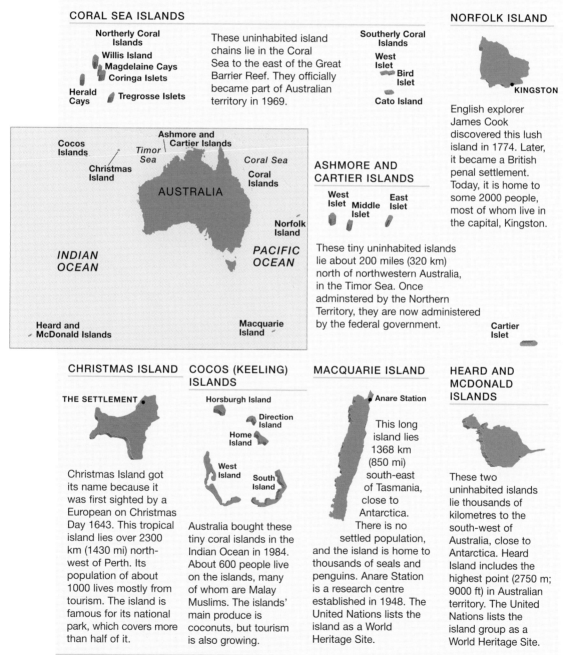

Cocos Islands
Timor Sea
Ashmore and Cartier Islands
Christmas Island
AUSTRALIA
Coral Sea
Coral Islands
Norfolk Island
INDIAN OCEAN
PACIFIC OCEAN
Heard and McDonald Islands
Macquarie Island

ASHMORE AND CARTIER ISLANDS

West Islet   Middle Islet   East Islet

These tiny uninhabited islands lie about 200 miles (320 km) north of northwestern Australia, in the Timor Sea. Once adminstered by the Northern Territory, they are now administered by the federal government.

Cartier Islet

CHRISTMAS ISLAND

THE SETTLEMENT

Christmas Island got its name because it was first sighted by a European on Christmas Day 1643. This tropical island lies over 2300 km (1430 mi) north-west of Perth. Its population of about 1000 lives mostly from tourism. The island is famous for its national park, which covers more than half of it.

COCOS (KEELING) ISLANDS

Horsburgh Island
Direction Island
Home Island
West Island
South Island

Australia bought these tiny coral islands in the Indian Ocean in 1984. About 600 people live on the islands, many of whom are Malay Muslims. The islands' main produce is coconuts, but tourism is also growing.

MACQUARIE ISLAND

Anare Station

This long island lies 1368 km (850 mi) south-east of Tasmania, close to Antarctica. There is no settled population, and the island is home to thousands of seals and penguins. Anare Station is a research centre established in 1948. The United Nations lists the island as a World Heritage Site.

HEARD AND MCDONALD ISLANDS

These two uninhabited islands lie thousands of kilometres to the south-west of Australia, close to Antarctica. Heard Island includes the highest point (2750 m; 9000 ft) in Australian territory. The United Nations lists the island group as a World Heritage Site.

AUSTRALIA'S CLIMATE

Because Australia is so vast, it is hardly surprising to discover that it has a wide range of climates, from the steamy wet season of the tropical north and the freezing temperatures and snowfalls of the south-eastern mountains, to the blazing heat of the desert interior. Most of Australia, however, is warm and dry throughout the year. More than two-thirds of the country receives too little rain for farming. In many of the remaining areas, the rain that does fall is too irregular and unevenly distributed to be of use to agriculture.

Bushfires

Australia's high temperatures can result in devastating bushfires that can destroy vast areas of vegetation. They are called 'bushfires' because they occur in rural areas, called the **bush** by Australians.

In the southern states, the worst bushfires usually burn during hot, dry summers. Many are caused by lightning strikes. Bushfires usually begin at ground level when conditions are hot, dry and windy and spread up tree trunks. The flames then jump from the crown of one tree to another. Hot currents of air carry burning embers over large distances, causing fresh fires where they land.

Bushfires are most common in eucalyptus forests. Unfortunately, these forests often lie in populated areas. The worst bushfires in Australian history occurred in Victoria on Friday 13 January 1939, which is remembered as Black Friday. In a single day, 71 people died in a blaze that destroyed 1300 buildings.

Botanists now believe that bushfires play a natural role in the life cycle of many Australian plants. Eucalyptus trees burn fiercely but grow back again after a fire. The seeds of some plants, such as banksias, open and germinate only after exposure to the heat of a bushfire.

Northern Australia is north of the Tropic of Capricorn – a line of latitude about 23.5 degrees south of the Equator – and has warm temperatures all year-round. South of this latitude, summers can still be very hot, but winters are cool. Generally, though, it is only in the eastern highlands that winter temperatures fall below freezing.

Darwin in the far north of Australia experiences a very different climate from Sydney in the south.

The lowest temperature recorded in Australia was at Charlotte Pass, New South Wales. It was –22 °C (–8 °F). The country's highest-recorded temperature was 53.1 °C (127.5 °F), at Cloncurry, Queensland. The most consistently hot place in Australia is Marble Bar, in northwestern Western Australia. The January average temperature is 41 °C (106 °F), and prolonged heat waves, where the temperature exceeds 40 °C (104 °F) for several weeks, are common.

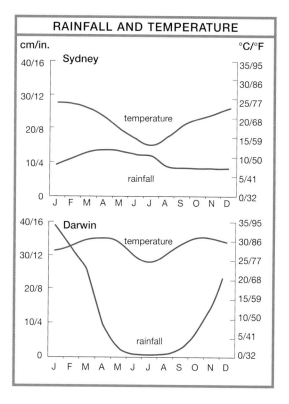

ANIMALS AND PLANTS

Australia was once part of a huge landmass that included Africa, Madagascar, India, Antarctica, New Zealand and South America. It began separating about 100 million years ago. Evidence that Australia once was joined to other continents can be found in the many plants and animals that have close relatives in these other places. For example, the Antarctic beech is found in Australia, New Zealand and Antarctica. At the same time, though, Australia's separation from other continents resulted in the evolution of unique flora and fauna.

Before the arrival of the Europeans some two hundred years ago, the Aborigines had already had a great effect on the environment. Because they survived by hunting,

The koala is a picky eater and will accept only a few species of eucalyptus leaves. In some areas of Australia, the koala is endangered because of the loss of its natural habitat and, therefore, of its preferred diet.

they often deliberately set fire to the natural vegetation to flush out their prey. By making these fires, they influenced the kinds of plants that were able to grow.

The impact of the Europeans, however, was much greater and far more destructive. The **colonists** introduced many non-native species of plants and animals. They also raised millions of sheep and cattle, which grazed the grassland areas, and cleared vast tracts of land to make way for European crops. As a consequence, many native plant and animal species became extinct or endangered. Many Australians today are worried about the loss of native habitats and wildlife, and the government has responded by setting up national parks to protect what remains of these fragile lands and wildlife species (see page 41).

Monotremes and marsupials

Australia is still home to many plants and animals that are very different from those found in other countries. Egg-laying mammals, or **monotremes**, for example, are found only in Australia and New Guinea, to Australia's north. Although monotremes are mammals, they lay soft-shelled eggs and suckle their young with milk that comes from ducts, not nipples. There are only two species of egg-laying mammals in the world – the platypus and the echidna. The platypus is found only in Australia, and it is Australia's most unusual animal.

The platypus lives in rivers and streams and has dense, waterproof fur, webbed feet and a bill like a duck. Echidnas are native to Australia and New Guinea. They are covered in long spines and also have fur. They eat ants and termites and use their long tongue to capture their prey from nests.

Marsupials are the main type of mammal in Australia. Marsupials are also found in South America but are far less widespread there. Marsupials give birth to underdeveloped young, which then climb into the mother's pouch to continue growing for some time.

In total, there are 144 species of marsupials in Australia.

Many types of marsupials, including the koala, make their home only in Australia. Other marsupials that are found in Australia include wallabies – a type of small kangaroo – wombats, possums and bandicoots. Possums are quite common and even nest in suburban gardens.

Only a few marsupials are carnivorous (meat-eaters). These once included the Tasmanian tiger, which is now believed to be extinct. Another carnivorous marsupial is the fierce Tasmanian devil. It is about the size of a badger and is jet-black, except for a white stripe on its chest. It comes out at night and preys on small birds and mammals. Its eerie whine can sometimes be heard during the night.

The red kangaroo

The red kangaroo is the kangaroo species most common to Central Australia. The males are called 'big reds' because they are taller than humans when standing. They usually lie in the shade during the day, but at times the males fight by balancing on their tails and kicking with their powerful hind legs. Their long toenails can cause deep wounds.

Female red kangaroos can delay breeding. During droughts, the embryo does not grow. As with all marsupials, when a baby kangaroo is born, it is not fully formed. It climbs into its mother's pouch, where it grows for about 190 days before it is big enough to live outside.

A popular Australian expression is 'as dumb as galahs'. A galah is a pink and grey parrot that has a reputation for being stupid.

Australia also has some native placental mammals; that is, mammals, like humans, that develop in the womb and are fully formed at birth. Of these, the most famous is the **dingo** – Australia's native dog – which arrived on the continent about 3000 or 4000 years ago. It was probably brought to Australia by traders from the north and was domesticated by Aboriginal people. Unlike domestic dogs, it howls rather than barks. Its eerie howl is a familiar sound in the Outback.

Colourful birds

There are about 740 species of birds in Australia. Of those, about 60 per cent are native. The emu and the cassowary, both flightless, are the largest birds. The emu, at 2 metres (6½ feet) tall, is also the second-largest bird in the world after the African ostrich.

Male bowerbirds are known for their unusual mating practice. They build elaborate bowers, or conical nests, to impress females and use flowers, berries and other objects of different colours to decorate the bowers.

The 55 species of parrots in Australia form the most colourful group of birds. Rainbow lorikeets, true to their name, have feathers that are coloured orange, red, blue, green and yellow. Also in the parrot group are budgerigars, which are famous as a caged bird throughout the world. In inland Australia, they can be seen flying in tightly packed flocks.

One of the best-known birds in Australia is the laughing kookaburra. It has a loud, cackling laugh and is the largest bird in the kingfisher family.

Rainbow lorikeets are members of the parrot family. They can be found in many parts of Australia, including city parks. At dusk, they gather in flocks in treetops and squawk loudly before settling down for the night. In urban areas, they can become quite tame and will land on a person's arm or shoulder to accept food. They feed on nectar from flowers.

Wildlife of the deep

Australia is famous for its sharks, though there are few shark attacks on humans. The most dangerous is the great white shark, which is found off the south coast. The whale shark is the largest, but it is harmless to humans. The Great Barrier Reef is home to some of the

world's most colourful fish, and about two hundred species of freshwater fish live in rivers and streams, mostly in Queensland's coastal rivers.

Other marine life that can be found in coastal waters includes humpback whales, turtles, dugongs – a type of sea-cow – and dolphins.

The wrasse is one of the many brightly coloured fish that make their home among the coral of the Great Barrier Reef.

Dangers in the wild

Australia is also home to many species of reptiles, including crocodiles, turtles, tortoises, lizards and snakes. Crocodiles are the largest living reptile in Australia and

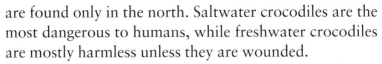

Australia has about 1500 species of ants – about 10% of the world total. One of the biggest is the bull-dog ant, which can be over 3 cm (1 in) long.

are found only in the north. Saltwater crocodiles are the most dangerous to humans, while freshwater crocodiles are mostly harmless unless they are wounded.

Some of the most dangerous snakes in the world are found in Australia. There are about 110 species of Australian snakes, and about half of these are venomous. The taipan and the tiger snake are the deadliest of the Australian snakes, although death adders, copperheads, brown snakes and red-bellied black snakes can also be dangerous to humans. Goannas are Australian lizards that can grow up to 2 metres (6 1/2 feet) long. They can be very aggressive and will hiss loudly if disturbed.

Australia also has some of the world's deadliest spiders. The funnel-web spider's bite can be fatal to humans. They are large, aggressive spiders, found mostly in New South Wales, and will actually run after their prey, including people, when disturbed. Redback spiders live in woodpiles and sheds, and their bite can be lethal.

The elegant Darling lily blooms in the dry, red soil of the Australian Outback.

Flowers in the desert

Australian plants are considered to be unique in the world, and many plant species are native to Australia. The vegetation is dominated by two large groups of plants – eucalypts (gum trees) and acacias (wattles) – which together have more than 1000 species. Most of Australia's original woodland has been cleared to make way for farming and grazing. Dense tropical rainforests and mangrove swamps grow in the wet and humid far north.

In the dry regions, plants have developed unusual ways of surviving long droughts. River red gums grow in Central Australia above underground water sources. Ghost gums have white bark to reflect the heat. More than 2000 species of wildflowers are able to thrive in the hot deserts of Western Australia, where there is little moisture.

National parks and World Heritage Sites

Since European settlement, the Australian landscape has changed dramatically. Experts estimate that within two centuries, Australia has lost 70% of its vegetation, including 40% of its forests. Even today, land clearing takes place at an alarming rate – every year, another 600,000 ha (1,480,000 acres) of native vegetation is lost.

Nevertheless, despite its generally poor environmental record, Australia has one of the world's largest networks of national parks – areas of protected wilderness. In total, there are some 500 national parks, ranging from vast tracts of empty Outback and rugged mountains to rainforests and coastal dunes. The map below shows some of the largest and best known of Australia's national parks.

The United Nations has listed thirteen areas within Australia as World Heritage Sites – natural or cultural places of global value. These include the Uluru (see page 30) and Kakadu (see page 29) national parks (listed as one site), the Great Barrier Reef, the fossil caves at Naracoorte, the rainforest reserves of New South Wales, the tiny **subtropical** Lord Howe Island and two of Australia's External Territories (see page 33).

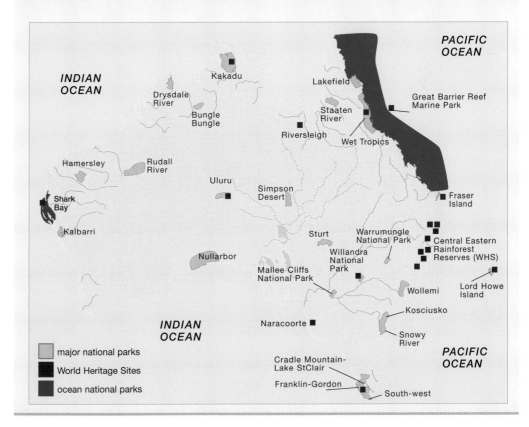

PACIFIC OCEAN

INDIAN OCEAN

Kakadu

Lakefield

Great Barrier Reef Marine Park

Drysdale River

Bungle Bungle

Staaten River

Riversleigh

Wet Tropics

Hamersley

Rudall River

Uluru

Simpson Desert

Shark Bay

Fraser Island

Kalbarri

Sturt

Warrumungle National Park

Central Eastern Rainforest Reserves (WHS)

Willandra National Park

Nullarbor

Mallee Cliffs National Park

Wollemi

Lord Howe Island

Kosciusko

INDIAN OCEAN

Naracoorte

Snowy River

PACIFIC OCEAN

☐ major national parks

■ World Heritage Sites

■ ocean national parks

Cradle Mountain-Lake StClair

Franklin-Gordon

South-west

41

AUSTRALIA'S CITIES

Since European settlement, most Australians have preferred to live in cities and towns, so that the vast interior region remains sparsely populated. Australia is one of the world's most urbanized countries in terms of where its population lives.

This view of Canberra shows the Australian War Memorial in the foreground, Lake Burley Griffin and the New Parliament House on Capital Hill in the background.

Canberra: the national capital

Canberra is a modern city, with grand public buildings, huge parklands and green, comfortable suburbs. It is unique in Australia not only because of its role as the national centre of government and administration, but also because it was carefully planned from the beginning, as opposed to expanding around a colonial town.

When the six British colonies in Australia became one nation – the Commonwealth of Australia – on 1 January 1901, they had to have a national capital (see page 8). So intense was the rivalry between Sydney and Melbourne for this honour that the best solution was to create a new city. The land for this city forms the Australian Capital Territory (ACT), and is situated about one-third of the way from Sydney to Melbourne. The ACT is similar to the District of Columbia in the United States, in that both are federal districts that contain the national capital.

To plan the capital, the Australian government held an international design competition in 1912. The winning design was by American landscape architect Walter Burley Griffin (1876–1937), whose plan allowed for a city of 25,000 people. Today, more than 300,000 people live in Canberra. As the population has grown, the original design has been maintained in the inner city, and newer areas have been planned along the same principles.

Most of Canberra has been built since the 1960s. The capital was officially named on 12 March 1913 – a day still celebrated as Canberra Day. A temporary Parliament House was opened in 1927, but there was little development in the next two decades because of the **Great Depression** and World War Two. In 1963, an artificial lake, called Lake Burley Griffin, was created by damming the Molonglo River. This lake is the city's centrepiece. Canberra grew rapidly up to the early 1990s, but since then its growth has stagnated because of cuts in the numbers of public servants and the relocation of some government departments to other cities. The city's main problem, however, is that it has little industry apart from administration and tourism.

Two million people visit the city every year. Its vast plantings of European trees and its many gardens are at their best in spring and autumn. The city is surrounded by rolling pastures and bushland and is flanked to the south-west by the hills of the Brindabella Ranges, which are capped with snow in winter.

Canberra's main attractions are around Lake Burley Griffin. On the lakeshore the national institutions are housed in some of Australia's most attractive buildings. Among the major sights are the New Parliament House (see page 79), completed in 1988, the Australian National

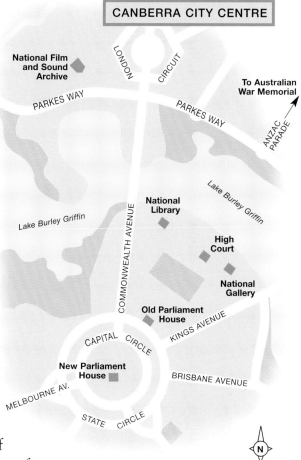

CANBERRA CITY CENTRE

National Film and Sound Archive
LONDON CIRCUIT
PARKES WAY
To Australian War Memorial
PARKES WAY
ANZAC PARADE
Lake Burley Griffin
National Library
Lake Burley Griffin
COMMONWEALTH AVENUE
High Court
National Gallery
Old Parliament House
KINGS AVENUE
CAPITAL CIRCLE
New Parliament House
BRISBANE AVENUE
MELBOURNE AV.
STATE CIRCLE
N

Australia's capital was laid out as a garden city, based around a central lake and surrounded by triangles of avenues. The city is dominated by monumental buildings that house national institutions, such as Parliament, the High Court and the National Art Gallery.

The Australian War Memorial

The Australian War Memorial in Canberra has a special place in Australia's national identity. It is an awe-inspiring, massive domed structure at the base of Mount Ainslie, a peak to the north-east of the city. From the memorial's steps, there is an uninterrupted view down Anzac Parade to the New Parliament House. The building serves as a memorial, museum, art gallery and library.

The memorial is Australia's tribute to the 110,000 Australians who have died in wars over the past 130 years. Opened in 1941, it houses relics of all wars in which Australians have served, and has a huge collection of art, photographs and written and audiovisual materials. These collections form a valuable part of Australia's national heritage.

More than a million people from all over the world visit the memorial each year. The commemorative area includes the Roll of Honour, which features the names of Australians who died in war inscribed on bronze plaques.

University, the National Library, the National Gallery, the National Film and Sound Archives, the High Court of Australia and the Australian War Memorial (see box).

Adelaide

Adelaide is the capital of South Australia, with a population of about 1 million people. It is a city with many churches and elegant colonial buildings. The variety of cafés, restaurants, theatres and other places of entertainment give Adelaide a lively atmosphere. Its reputation as a centre of culture is based on its biennial (every other year) Adelaide Arts Festival, which attracts performers from all over the world.

Its sunny weather and broad, tree-lined streets give Adelaide's city centre something of a European atmosphere, but it is now home to people from all over the

Adelaide was named after Queen Adelaide, the wife of King William IV (1765–1837), king of England.

world. Despite its lively atmosphere, though, it still has some of the feel of a large country town. Life in Adelaide is much more relaxed than in Australia's larger cities.

Adelaide's city centre is surrounded by green parkland, and the metropolitan area is flanked by the hills of the Mount Lofty Ranges. The Torrens River flows to the north of the city centre.

The site for Adelaide was chosen in 1836, and it was begun as a planned city in a model **colony**. A model colony was one that was meant to be free of the problems experienced by other Australian settlements, such as crime. It swiftly established the reputation of being a tolerant place. Europeans suffering religious persecution were encouraged to settle around Adelaide in the mid-19th century.

For much of the 20th century, the city came to be regarded as a rather old-fashioned, backward-looking place, known more for its churches than its social life. However, in the 1970s, under a newly elected **premier** (head of state government), Don Dunstan (1926–99), Adelaide gained a new reputation for promoting better welfare benefits for the poor and disadvantaged and for encouraging the arts.

On North Terrace are the Old Parliament House, casino, hotels, museum, art gallery, the University of South Australia and the Botanic Gardens. Parklands and the Torrens River separate the city centre from the historic houses of the North Adelaide district.

Adelaide is a spacious, green city that straddles the Torrens River. It has broad, well-planned streets that are laid out on a grid system.

ADELAIDE CITY CENTRE

NORTH ADELAIDE

ZOO

Adelaide Oval

MONTEFIORE ROAD

KING WILLIAM ROAD

FROME ROAD

Torrens River

Festival Centre

University of Adelaide

Botanic Gardens

museum

NORTH TERRACE

casino

Old Parliament House

State Library

art gallery

University of South Australia

HINDLEY STREET

CURRIE STREET

GAWLER STREET

PULTNEY STREET

FROME STREET

WAYMOUTH STREET

FRANKLIN STREET

GROTE STREET

Central Market

GOUGER STREET

N

Sydney was named after Viscount Sydney, an 18th-century British politician.

Sydney

When Governor Arthur Phillip (1738–1814) landed at Sydney Cove in 1788 to found the first British colony in Australia, he called the harbour, Port Jackson, the finest in the world. More than two hundred years later, few would disagree with that verdict. Sydney's harbour, coastline, bays, inlets and the Parramatta River, which flows into the harbour, give the city its international reputation as the gateway to Australia.

Sydney has an enormous variety of restaurants, bars, theatres and music and sporting venues. And it is a city of great contrasts. Its 4 million people, rich and poor, come from every part of the world. Immigrants have enriched Sydney's culture, and today it is very much a bustling, cosmopolitan city.

Sydney is an exciting city to explore, especially by ferry. Circular Quay, between the southern end of the great Sydney Harbour Bridge and the magnificent Sydney Opera House, is the hub of Sydney's water transportation system. From here, ferries cruise the harbour and take passengers as far as Manly, a northern suburb, and Parramatta, a western suburb.

Much of Sydney's skyline and that of North Sydney, across the harbour, is now dominated by skyscrapers and is constantly changing with the construction of new buildings. As the host city of the 2000 Olympics,

Sydney's city centre area borders the magnficent harbour. On the left are the Sydney Harbour Bridge, known affectionately by Sydneysiders as 'The Coathanger', and Luna Park, an amusement park.

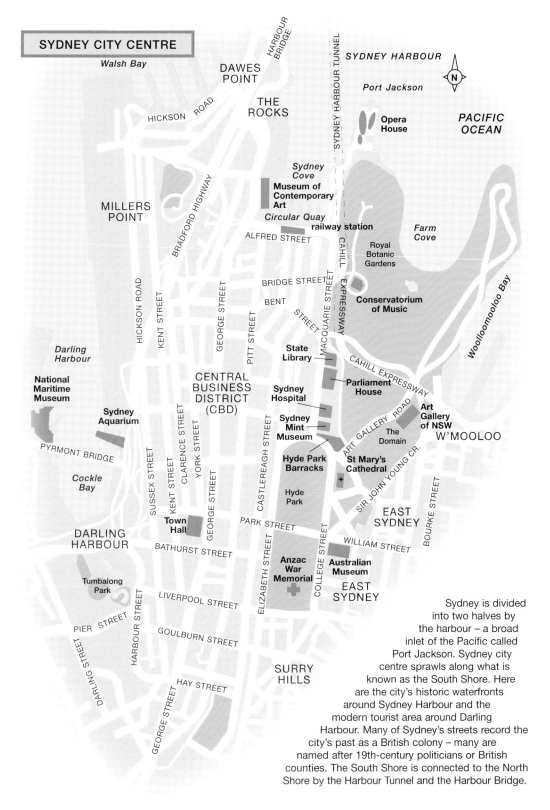

SYDNEY CITY CENTRE

Walsh Bay

HARBOUR BRIDGE

SYDNEY HARBOUR TUNNEL

SYDNEY HARBOUR

DAWES POINT

Port Jackson

N

THE ROCKS

HICKSON ROAD

Opera House

PACIFIC OCEAN

Sydney Cove

Museum of Contemporary Art

BRADFORD HIGHWAY

MILLERS POINT

Circular Quay

railway station

Farm Cove

ALFRED STREET

CAHILL EXPRESSWAY

Royal Botanic Gardens

HICKSON ROAD

KENT STREET

GEORGE STREET

BRIDGE STREET

BENT

STREET

MACQUARIE STREET

Conservatorium of Music

PITT STREET

Darling Harbour

State Library

CAHILL EXPRESSWAY

Woolloomooloo Bay

National Maritime Museum

CENTRAL BUSINESS DISTRICT (CBD)

Sydney Hospital

Parliament House

ART GALLERY ROAD

Art Gallery of NSW

Sydney Aquarium

CLARENCE STREET

YORK STREET

CASTLEREAGH STREET

Sydney Mint Museum

The Domain

W'MOOLOO

PYRMONT BRIDGE

SUSSEX STREET

KENT STREET

GEORGE STREET

Hyde Park Barracks

St Mary's Cathedral

Cockle Bay

Hyde Park

SIR JOHN YOUNG CR.

EAST SYDNEY

BOURKE STREET

Town Hall

PARK STREET

DARLING HARBOUR

BATHURST STREET

GEORGE STREET

ELIZABETH STREET

COLLEGE STREET

WILLIAM STREET

Tumbalong Park

LIVERPOOL STREET

Anzac War Memorial

Australian Museum

EAST SYDNEY

PIER STREET

HARBOUR STREET

GOULBURN STREET

DARLING STREET

HAY STREET

GEORGE STREET

SURRY HILLS

Sydney is divided into two halves by the harbour – a broad inlet of the Pacific called Port Jackson. Sydney city centre sprawls along what is known as the South Shore. Here are the city's historic waterfronts around Sydney Harbour and the modern tourist area around Darling Harbour. Many of Sydney's streets record the city's past as a British colony – many are named after 19th-century politicians or British counties. The South Shore is connected to the North Shore by the Harbour Tunnel and the Harbour Bridge.

Sydney experienced a building boom, and there was much redevelopment of its public spaces. The main site for the Olympics was Homebush Bay on the Parramatta River, where an old industrial site was converted to a modern Olympic village.

One of the areas redeveloped in the late 1980s was Darling Harbour. This waterside leisure park is a show-piece of the city. From Darling Harbour, it is just a short walk to Sydney's Chinatown, a centre of Chinese-Australian culture.

The best way to appreciate the old part of Sydney is on foot. The Rocks, an area lying beneath the southern end of the Sydney Harbour Bridge, is rich in history. In the 19th century and the early 20th century, it was noto-rious for its slums and the 'larrikin' (unruly) gangs who terrorized its streets. In the 1830s and 1840s, many fine sandstone warehouses were built there.

The historic buildings have since been restored and renovated, and today the Rocks is one of Sydney's major attractions. It has fine old pubs, galleries, cafés, muse-ums and a street market every weekend for arts and crafts.

Sydney's Hyde Park provides a green and tranquil haven for people who work in the city centre. Many office workers take their lunch break here, away from the noise and fumes of the traffic.

In and near Macquarie Street, some of Sydney's most important historic buildings have been restored and preserved. There is the Mint, St Mary's Cathedral, the Public Library of New South Wales, Parliament House, the Conservatorium of Music and Hyde Park Barracks, which was designed by a convict architect in 1817–19 to house convict work gangs. In this part of Sydney, there are also the green, open spaces of Hyde Park, the Domain and the fine Royal Botanic Gardens.

Melbourne

With a population of about 3 million, Melbourne is Australia's second-largest city after Sydney, and has a reputation for being the cultural, food and fashion capital of the country.

First settled in 1837, the city was the centre of Australia's biggest gold rush from the 1850s, which saw a period of great prosperity. The wealth poured into Melbourne, which became known at that time as 'Marvellous Melbourne'.

Melbourne is graced with plentiful parks and gardens, wide, tree-lined streets and stately buildings dating from the Victorian era (1837–1901), as well as gleaming skyscrapers. It is home to people who have migrated from all over the world and is a lively, cosmopolitan city that has much to offer the visitor. The city centre is located on the banks of the Yarra River, while the suburbs spread out around the shores of Port Phillip Bay, about 5 kilometres (3 miles) from the city centre.

One of the best ways to see Melbourne is by tram. These relics from the past crisscross the city and the inner suburbs, ringing their bells and creating a colourful sight wherever they go. Along the banks of the Yarra River are cycle tracks that lead out of the city centre into numerous parks.

Spring Street has some of Melbourne's finest buildings, including the State Houses of Parliament. This building was built with gold-rush wealth and housed the national parliament while Canberra was being built. Also in the centre are some impressive churches.

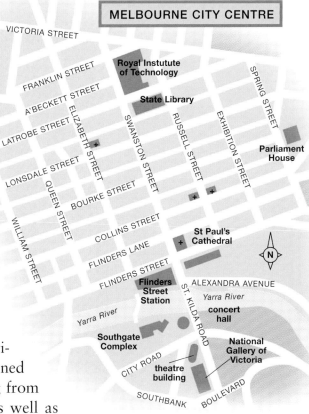

Melbourne's main natural feature is the muddy Yarra River. The city centre lies to the north of the Yarra.

Past and present

'The earth and sea of their own accord furnish them with all the things necessary for Life ...'

Captain James Cook, 1770, on Australia's Aborigines

For about 40,000 years, Australia's **Aboriginal peoples** developed their societies in isolation. In 1788, however, the British began to colonize Australia, and European **immigration** to the continent began.

The first **colonies** were started as places to send Britain's unwanted prison population, rather like large jails. Most convicts were imprisoned for seven years. After they had served their sentences, ex-convicts, or emancipists, soon became a large part of the population. Other free settlers included the soldiers and government officials who had migrated to the new colonies with the convicts. Wealthy people soon followed, attracted by the new opportunities. Starting in 1831, skilled workers in Britain and Ireland were being encouraged to migrate to the Australian colonies.

By the 1850s, most of the colonies had achieved self-government and had become prosperous through exporting wool and gold mining. However, the land that the British settlers claimed had originally been Aboriginal land. The **colonists** had little respect for the Aborigines' way of life. It was only in the 1960s that Australia began to right the wrongs done to its first peoples.

The history of Australia as a nation began when the six colonies became states of the new Commonwealth of Australia in 1901. However, it was several decades before Australia became completely independent.

From time to time, Aborigines returned to the same place to make and trade their stone tools. They left the ground scattered with stone fragments.

FACT FILE

- Aborigines lived in Australia for thousands of years before the first European settlers arrived. Experts debate how long ago the Aborigines arrived in the continent – some claim as long as 60,000 years ago; others claim 40,000 years ago.

- In 1606, the Dutch ship *Duyfken* became the first European vessel to land in Australia. The Dutch called the land 'New Holland' after a province of the Netherlands.

- Australia's British colonists justified their claims to its territory by arguing that it was *terra nullius* – 'no one's land'.

> 'I want people to change their attitudes to Aboriginal people. I want Australians to have pride in a culture that is practically the oldest culture in the world.'
> – Aboriginal storyteller Ninjali Josie Lawford

ANCIENT AUSTRALIA

Aboriginal peoples probably migrated to Australia from Asia during the last Ice Age, some 40,000 years ago. At that time, the level of the seas was much lower than it is today, and people could travel from South-East Asia to the Australian continent by walking across the land and crossing narrow seas in canoes.

A changing continent, changing lifestyles

Over many thousands of years, early Aboriginal peoples had to adapt to great changes. We know from fossils and archaeological evidence that, 40,000 years ago, Australia was a very different place from what it is today. The continent was covered in forests, and there were huge inland lakes that teemed with fish. Many of the megafauna (huge animals) still roamed the country, including 3-metre (10-feet) tall kangaroos and flightless birds.

Then, some 15,000 years ago, the Ice Age came to an end. The temperature rose, the ice melted and great chunks of coastal land were flooded. Australia became an isolated island. The inland lakes dried up, and vast deserts were formed. As the inland became more inhospitable, many Aborigines migrated to the coast.

The Aboriginal people learned how to survive in even the harshest environment. They learned to grind stone to make better axes. They also developed the boomerang, spear and woven nets to trap wallabies and kangaroos. The Aborigines' main tool, however, was a sharp stick, used to dig out roots and small

Aboriginal languages

When the Europeans arrived in Australia in 1788, there were probably about 250 Aboriginal languages and many more **dialects**. Experts think that these developed from a single parent language. Traditionally, most Aborigines spoke two or more languages.

Since European contact, the number of Aboriginal languages has declined. Today, only about 30 languages are spoken. Aboriginal Kriol is a language that has developed since the Europeans arrived. It uses a mixture of English and Aboriginal words. Some Aboriginal words have entered English, including *kangaroo* and *boomerang*. The name 'Kylie' is an Aboriginal word for a small boomerang.

Australia's first peoples

Although Aboriginal peoples were **nomadic**, they had a strong attachment to their homelands. Unlike the Europeans, who usually settled on the fertile coasts, the Aborigines occupied the entire continent. In all, there may have been about five hundred different Aboriginal groups.

This map shows the distribution of the larger groups in Australia before European settlement began in 1788.

TIWI
MAUNG
LARAKIA
MURNGIN
KAKADJU
BRINKEN
NUNGGUBUYU
WUNDAMBAL
MARA
WIK-MUNKAN
YIR YORONT
UNGARINYIN
BARD
GUIRINDJI
NYUL-NYUL
KARADJERI
NJANGOMADA
MANDJILDJARA
WALBIRI
WORKIA
KARIERA
NGALIA
WAKELBURA
BINDUBI
MUDBARA
ARANDA
GADUDJARA
BIDJANDJARA
(PITJANTATJARA)
ANDINGARI
TURRBAL
BUDIDJARA
DIERI
KUMBAINGERI
MIRNING
KAMILAROI
WHADJUK
BANGGALA
WAKELBURA
WURADJERI
BIBELMAN
GAURNA
KAMERAIGAL
WURUNJERRI

animals from the earth. While hunting was mainly the responsibility of men, food gathering was carried out by women.

Aborigines enjoyed a good variety of foods. While meat was a preferred food, they also ate fruits, nuts, roots, fungi and insects. Grubs and ants provided the Aborigines with a valuable source of sugars and fats. Most foods were eaten raw. Meat, though, was roasted over an open fire or in a simple oven – a shallow pit filled with hot coals. Water was very precious, and Aborigines knew exactly where to find it. Sometimes they cut off the roots of certain trees and shrubs that held water.

Between 3000 and 4000 years ago, the **dingo**, Australia's native dog, arrived in the country. It was probably brought by traders from Asia. The Aborigines trained the dingo to help them hunt by chasing kangaroos and sniffing out burrowing animals.

Groups and territories

Towards the end of the 18th century, there were probably around 750,000 Aboriginal people in Australia. They belonged to different groups whose members shared the same language (see page 52). A group would also hunt together and practise the same religion. Different groups traded with each other and exchanged technologies and ideas.

Within each group, the people moved about in smaller bands. In each band, the important decisions were made by its elders. The boundaries of each group were established by its creation stories – stories that told of the group's spirit ancestors – so they never tried to take each other's land. When there was conflict between groups, it was usually over ceremonial problems, customs or the belief that one group had used sorcery (magic) against another. Conflicts were usually settled by the elders.

Mother-of-pearl pendants such as this one were traded by Aborigines across vast distances. This 20th-century one comes from the Kimberley region in Western Australia.

A Dreaming story of Uluru

The story goes that **Uluru** (see page 30) was created by two boys playing in mud left by the rain. These boys were the spirit ancestors of the people who now own Uluru. The mound of mud they built became the great rock. After a while, the two boys went hunting. One threw a club at a wallaby. His club missed but struck the earth, causing a spring of water to gush forth. He was selfish and did not tell the older boy about this spring. Dying of thirst, the second boy began to fight with the first. Both were changed into boulders and can still be seen on top of Atila, a nearby plateau.

The Dreamtime

Aboriginal people believe that the land and all the natural features of the world were created by supernatural ancestral beings in a time before the arrival of humans. They call this time the **Dreamtime**. These spirit ancestors continue to exist in the landscape. They influence natural events and give life to all living things. Totems are the link between the spirit ancestors and the people, and every person has his or her own totem. Totems are usually animals, and can take the form of a wallaby, bird or fish, for instance.

The Dreaming, or creation, stories gave each Aboriginal group its customs, laws and rituals and were handed down from one generation to the next. Each group's stories related to its own area of land. They explained how features of the land were made and how living things got their characteristics. They also told of the best times and places to hunt or fish, and where to find water when there was a drought. They gave lessons about how to behave, and offered guidance on how a person should choose a suitable marriage partner.

Rooted in the land

The Dreaming stories also explain why individuals did not own land. Land had a religious, or sacred, meaning, and each group belonged to its land as much as the land belonged to the group. The most important parts of the land were sacred sites. These were the places, such as a tree, hill or rocky outcrop (see page 14), where the spirit ancestors lived and held life-giving powers.

Each person had a strong bond to the sacred site that was associated with his or her spirit ancestor. It was each person's responsibility to help care for a particular site by performing ceremonies and rituals and singing the songs that told of the spirit ancestor's activities in the Dreamtime. In this way, the natural order of things that the spirit ancestor created was maintained.

Aborigines in Arnhem Land in the Northern Territory use bark from the stringybark tree to paint on. This bark painting depicts two kangaroos and a lizard in an X-ray style.

The Greek Theopompus (born about 380 BC) spoke of 'a continent or parcel of dry land that is infinite in size', which lay to the south.

COLONIAL AUSTRALIA

Since ancient times, there had been legends in Europe and Asia about a great *Terra Australis Incognita* ('Unknown Southern Land'). The Chinese explorer Cheng Ho (*c.*1371 to *c.*1433) may have reached Australia in the mid-15th century, while Malay fishermen began to camp on the continent's northern shores in the 16th century. By this time, a vast southern landmass appeared on many European maps of the world.

The 'Unknown Southern Land'

In the 16th century, European navigators explored the Earth's southern oceans in search of the *Terra Australis.* The Dutch were probably the first to land in Australia, which they called New Holland. Its barren landscape discouraged any settlement, however. In the 1640s, the Dutch explorer Abel Tasman (1603–59) reached a more promising region. He called it Van Diemen's Land, but it was later renamed Tasmania in his honour.

Starting in the 17th century, Europeans began to explore the the oceans and land that lay to the south of South-East Asia.

While the Dutch explorations suggested the existence of a large landmass, 'New Holland' itself remained unknown. Indeed, it was not until 1803 that Australia was fully circumnavigated and its actual size determined. This time it was the British who led the way in exploring the unknown continent.

The first Englishman to arrive in Australia was a pirate called William Dampier (1652–1715), who landed in Shark's Bay on the west coast in 1688. Finally, in 1770, the English captain James Cook (see box opposite) landed several times on the fertile east coast of Australia. Cook called the land New South Wales and claimed it for Britain.

→ Abel Tasman 1642–4
→ William Dampier 1688
→ James Cook 1770

EARLY SEA EXPLORERS

PACIFIC OCEAN

Torres Strait

Possession Island   Cape York

Great Barrier Reef

Shark's Bay

NEW SOUTH WALES

Botany Bay

Point Hicks

N

INDIAN OCEAN

Tasmania

The voyage of the *Endeavour*

In 1768, the British government organized the first scientific expedition to the Pacific. In charge of the expedition was the 40-year-old sea captain James Cook, and onboard his ship, the *Endeavour*, was a team of distinguished scientists, naturalists, astronomers and artists whose job was to research and record the expedition's discoveries. Their special mission, however, was to find the *Terra Australis*, the 'Southern Land', a great continent that scientists believed existed.

Cook's first landfall was New Zealand. From there, he sailed westwards and struck Australia's unexplored eastern coast. The first sight of land was the south-eastern tip of the continent, which Cook called Point Hicks. There was nowhere to land, however, and the ship headed north along the coast.

Another nine days passed before Cook found a suitable anchorage in a sheltered bay. Onshore, the scientists observed and recorded the wealth of strange plants and animals they found, giving the bay its name – Botany Bay (botany is the scientific study of plants). The naturalist Joseph Banks, who accompanied Cook, wrote: 'All things in this land seemed quaint and opposite'.

From Botany Bay, the *Endeavour* sailed north again. The green, fertile coastland was very different from Australia's other shores, which were dry and uninviting. The ship had to navigate the dangerous **Great Barrier Reef**, and eventually the ship was grounded just off the north Queensland coast, at present-day Cooktown. It took six weeks to repair the battered *Endeavour*, and once again the scientific team explored the coast.

Cook set sail again and rounded Australia's northern tip, Cape York. Shortly after, he landed on Possession Island, planted the Union Jack in the soil and claimed the whole territory for Britain – a scene that was commemorated in many paintings. Cook and the *Endeavour* returned triumphantly to England.

Clearing the woods

One of the captains of the eleven British ships that sailed to Australia in 1787 was David Collins. He wrote the following account of the earliest days of the settlement at Port Jackson: 'The spot chosen … was at the head of the cove near a run of fresh water … the stillness of which had then for the first time since creation been interrupted by the rude sound of the woods-man's axe … The spot which had so been lately the abode of silence and tranquillity was now changed to that of noise, clamour and confusion. As the woods were opened and the ground cleared, the encampments were extended and all wore the appearance of regularity.' Collin's description suggests that he thought of the British as bringing order to an untamed wilderness.

The first settlers

During the 18th century, thousands of British prisoners were sent to work in Britain's colonies in North America. However, after the American Revolutionary War (1775–83), Britain could no longer dispose of prisoners that way. As a result, British prisons became terribly overcrowded.

In 1786, the British government decided that New South Wales would make a suitable place for a convict colony – the climate and soil were good, the Aboriginal people did not pose a big threat and convicts would have nowhere to go even if they did manage to escape.

A fleet of eleven sailing ships left Britain on 13 May 1787, carrying 759 convicts and 206 marines to guard them. The voyage to Australia took more than eight months. The original plan had been to settle at Botany Bay. However, after arriving there on 18 January 1788, the poor harbour, unpromising soil and scarce water supplies forced the fleet to move on. Port Jackson to the

Convicts onboard ships to Australia suffered overcrowded and unhealthy conditions during the eight-month journey. Many of them died of disease before they even reached Australia.

north offered a much more promising harbour. The British flag was raised there on 26 January, and a colony was set up under the fleet's commander, Captain Arthur Phillip. Captain Phillip governed the colony from 1788 to 1792. This colony grew to become the city of Sydney.

More than 160,000 men, women and children were sent as convicts to New South Wales and, later, to most of the other Australian colonies as they were started. Some of these criminals were violent, but many had been forced to commit small crimes because of poverty at home in Britain. To try to reduce crime, the British government made almost 200 crimes punishable by death, but others were punished by long jail sentences. About one-fifth of those sentenced to jail were transported to Australia.

Life in a colony

The convicts' fate was largely a matter of luck. Some were well treated; some were not. Those with useful skills were usually set free early, but many other convicts suffered great cruelty. Some worked for the government. Others were assigned as servants for officers, free settlers and even ex-convicts.

As punishment for wrongdoing during their sentences, convicts could be put into chain gangs or sent to a penal settlement. These were terrible places where the most common punishment was being whipped with a cat-o'-nine-tails – a whip usually made of nine knotted lines tied to a handle.

Convicts who behaved well could receive a 'ticket-of-leave'. This meant they could work for themselves during the remainder of their sentences. A convict who received a conditional pardon was completely free but could not leave the colony. Some gained full pardons, which meant they were free to stay or to leave.

The battle of Vinegar Hill

At the beginning of the 19th century, the British government began to send captured Irish rebels to Australia. In 1804, many of these Irish convicts took part in an uprising that began at a government farm at Castle Hill, near Sydney. They planned to march to Sydney, seize some ships and escape. However, they were defeated on their way by soldiers at Vinegar Hill. Their leaders were hanged, and many others were whipped and sent to work in the coal mines of Newcastle on the east coast of Australia.

*As increasing numbers
of British settlers came
to Australia's new
cities, explorers were
venturing deeper
into the Outback.*

➤ Charles Sturt
1828–30,
1844–5
➤ Edward Eyre
1839–41
➤ Friedrich
Leichhardt
1844–5
➤ A. C. Gregory
1855–6,
1858
➤ John McDouall
Stuart
1859–62
➤ Burke and Wills
1860–1
➤ Warburton
1872–3

*This 1837 print shows
the site of Adelaide
as it would have
appeared to the early
settlers. A modern
and attractive city
has grown from
these rather
humble
beginnings.*

SETTLERS AND EXPLORERS

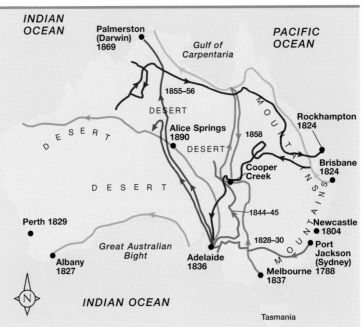

New colonies

After 1788, more British settlements were founded in
Australia. Van Diemen's Land became a separate colony
called Tasmania in 1825. Another convict settlement was
made at Moreton Bay in Brisbane in 1824. It became a
free settlement in 1842, and the separate colony of
Queensland was started in 1859. A convict colony was set
up at Albany in Western Australia in 1827 but was soon
abandoned. However, only two years later, a free settlement was begun on the site of modern Perth. Settlement
attempts in the **tropical** north were less successful. The
first permanent northern settlement, at Palmerston
(later named Darwin), was
not made until 1869.

The Burke and Wills expedition

In 1860, the South Australian parliament offered a £2000 reward to the first person who could establish an overland route from the south coast to the north. The race was on. The first to make the attempt was John McDouall Stuart (1815–66). By April, Stuart had reached the geographical centre of Australia, some 200 km (125 mi) north of Alice Springs. At this point, illness forced Stuart to retrace his steps. Undeterred, however, he soon set out again.

In August 1860, two more explorers, Robert O'Hara Burke (1821–61; shown here) and William John Wills (1834–61), and their party of eighteen men set out from Melbourne, in the south, to travel to the Gulf of Carpentaria, in the north. They took 24 camels, 28 horses and 21 tons of provisions. Unlike earlier explorers, however, they did not take Aboriginal guides. In November, they reached Cooper Creek in South Australia, where they left the other members of their party at a base camp. Burke and Wills and two members of their party continued on by camel (see page 95) for the Gulf of Carpentaria.

They managed to reach the gulf in 1861, and began the long journey home. One member of the party died, and the others delayed a day in order to bury him. Exhausted and almost out of food, Burke and Wills and the other member of their party, John King, managed to struggle back to Cooper Creek. By this time, they were about two months behind schedule, and the other members of their party had given up hope and moved on only hours before. They had left some provisions for the men, which they buried some distance from a tree with the message 'Dig under 40ft W'. But Burke and Wills never found the provisions, and both died of starvation.

King was the only member of the party to survive. He was looked after by the local Aboriginal people until he was later rescued by a search party. Stuart, meanwhile, finally reached Arnhem Land in July 1862 and returned home a hero.

Today, the 'Dig tree' still stands beside Cooper Creek, although the carved message has long since gone. There is a stone memorial beside the tree in memory of the tragic Burke and Wills.

Melbourne was not founded until 1837. The first settlements in the area were made by 'squatters', men who seized land for sheep grazing. Victoria became a separate colony from New South Wales in 1850. Unique among these colonies was South Australia. In 1837, it became the first colony to be settled by a completely free population – people who had chosen to travel to Australia rather than convicts who had been deported there.

Resistance and conflict

The British considered Australia *terra nullius*, the Latin term for 'no one's land'.

Colonization caused bloodshed. At the heart of the matter was control of land. The British did not recognize Aboriginal ownership of the country. Although the British government expressed concern about native rights, the local authorities sent soldiers against Aborigines. As settlement spread, there was conflict between settlers and Aborigines in one district after another.

Typically, settlers moved into an area and took land for grazing sheep or cattle. Aboriginal people resisted these incursions, spearing stock and attacking homesteads. Settlers reacted by organizing armed, mounted bands of men. These bands frequently massacred any Aboriginal people they came across. In Tasmania, almost the entire Aboriginal population was wiped out.

At least 20,000 Aborigines were killed by settlers in colonial times, ten times the number of whites killed by Aboriginal people. Survivors were reduced to living like slaves on land that had once been their own. By 1933, there were only about 70,000 Aborigines left in Australia.

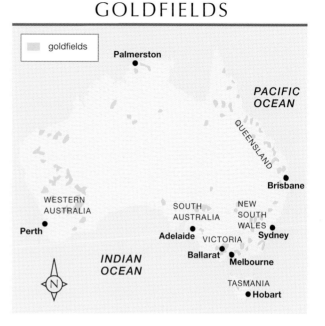

GOLDFIELDS

goldfields

Palmerston

PACIFIC OCEAN

QUEENSLAND

Brisbane

WESTERN AUSTRALIA

SOUTH AUSTRALIA

NEW SOUTH WALES

Perth

Adelaide

VICTORIA

Sydney

Ballarat

Melbourne

INDIAN OCEAN

TASMANIA

Hobart

The lure of gold

The events that did most to increase the non-Aboriginal population of Australia were the gold rushes that began in the early 1850s. People deserted their jobs, towns and ships to join the rush to be rich. They were soon joined by thousands of people from overseas.

Gold was found throughout Australia. In the mid-19th century, Ballarat in Victoria was the world's richest goldfield.

Mining, or panning, for alluvial gold required only simple equipment. It was often a hard life for the miners: they lived in tents called 'humpies', and the winters were often freezing cold.

The early discoveries were mostly alluvial gold – that is, traces of gold found in clay, sand or gravel deposited by running water. Only simple equipment was needed to explore for such gold. All of the prospectors had equal chances of making their fortunes, but life on the 'diggings' was hard. Most people never became rich and, as alluvial gold became scarce, mining became the business of companies with the money to sink deep mine shafts.

The goldfields were sometimes violent places. Thousands of Chinese diggers who came to Australia were met with hostility from Europeans, who sometimes tried to drive them off the goldfields. The worst race riots were at Lambing Flat in New South Wales in 1861 (see box).

The gold rushes brought many changes. Wealth from gold raised people's living standards, and wages rose as employers competed for workers. Britain stopped sending convicts to eastern Australia after 1853, but Australia's population increased by more than 300 per cent during the 1850s. Ten per cent of gold-rush migrants came from outside Britain and Ireland. Europeans were accepted, but some colonies passed laws that made it difficult for Asians to enter Australia.

The Lambing Flat riots

Many Chinese people were attracted to Australia by the wealth that could be made in the goldfields. However, there was considerable hostility towards the Chinese from the European diggers. In January 1861, at Lambing Flat in New South Wales, several thousand Chinese were driven from the goldfields by the diggers.

Troops arrived to try to control the situation, but in June 1861, 3000 Europeans took the law into their own hands and attacked the Chinese. There was a battle with mounted police and one miner died. Thirteen miners were arrested, but only one was convicted.

The Lambing Flat riots led to moves to restrict Chinese immigration. This was the beginning of the 'White Australia' policy (see page 68), which restricted Asian immigration.

The Eureka Stockade
One of the best-known events in Australian history occurred during the 1850s gold rush. This was the revolt at the Eureka Stockade at Ballarat, Victoria, in

1854. From 1851 to 1854, discontent had been rising over a number of issues in the goldfields. At the time, diggers were expected to pay a large fee for a licence to prospect. They received no police protection, transportation or road maintenance in return, and were not allowed to vote.

On 17 October 1854, Ballarat diggers formed the Ballarat Reform League. At that time, only wealthy adult men were allowed to vote and

The legend of the bushrangers

Some of the best-known characters in Australian history are **bushrangers**. According to legend, the bushrangers were Robin Hood-like people who had been wronged by the law, and who robbed the rich and were friends of the poor. Many people regarded the bushrangers as heroes.

The first bushrangers were escaped convicts who lived in the bush and robbed people to survive. The next main period of bushranging began during the gold rushes in the 1850s and lasted until the 1870s. Coaches carrying gold from the diggings became the target of bushrangers, who were nearly all from families of poor rural workers.

Ned Kelly (1855–80) and his gang were the most famous of the bushrangers. Ned's parents were poor farmers in Victoria. His father, Red Kelly, died in 1866, and Ellen Kelly, Ned's mother, was left to raise her children in poverty. When she was jailed in 1878, Ned and his brother Dan took up bushranging.

After many exploits, the Kelly gang fought their last battle in 1879, at Glenrowan in Victoria. As the police laid siege to the town, the gang donned iron masks made out of plough parts. All died in the battle except Ned, who was taken to Melbourne jail, tried and hanged. Ned in his iron mask has become a popular symbol of the Australian spirit.

be members of the Victorian parliament. The league called for votes for all adult men for members of the Victorian parliament, payment for members of parliament and an end to prospectors' licences and property requirements for members of parliament. These last demands were put forward so that people who were not rich could enter parliament.

On 29 November, 12,000 diggers met at Eureka, and many burned their licences in protest. They made a new flag of stars on a white cross against a blue background and swore to stand together. The diggers built a stockade (enclosure) at Eureka and collected weapons.

Before dawn on Sunday 3 December 1854, 270 soldiers and police attacked 150 diggers in the stockade and defeated the diggers in battle. Thirty diggers and five soldiers were killed. However, the diggers achieved most of their aims. Juries did not convict the thirteen ringleaders who were tried for treason, and in 1855 the gold licence was replaced by a miner's 'right', which cost one pound a year and gave its holder the right to vote.

New settlers often tried to make Australia as much like their old country as possible – for instance, they often hunted native animals as they would at home. This print from 1890 shows settlers driving stock (top), playing cricket (top right) and hunting kangaroos on horseback (bottom).

Changing colonial society

Perhaps surprisingly, the Australian colonies had become more **democratic** as a result of the gold rushes. Until that time, only wealthy white men could vote and become members of parliament. During the 1850s, the law changed, and all adult white men became eligible to vote for the lower house of parliament in South Australia, Victoria and New South Wales. In 1900, all white men in Tasmania were allowed to vote as well.

As in most countries, though, women did not get the right to vote until some time later. Adult white women could not vote until 1894 in South Australia, 1902 in New South Wales, 1903 in Tasmania and 1908 in Victoria. Aboriginal people of either sex could not vote until the 1960s in most states (see page 76).

Until the 1850s, the governors of each colony, who were appointed by the British government, could overrule any laws the parliaments tried to introduce. Starting in the 1850s, each of the Australian colonies gained the right to run its own affairs instead of acting on orders from Britain, although Britain still controlled the colonies' relations with the rest of the world.

From the bush to the city

Although many Australians thought of themselves as people of the **bush**, more and more began to live in towns or cities as the 19th century progressed. Wealthy squatters controlled the best lands, and most people who worked the land had only small farms. Trade unions (organizations that fought for better wages and conditions for workers) were first formed among skilled workers in the towns and later among sheepshearers and other bush workers.

In the prosperous 1870s and 1880s, these unions won many improvements for the workers. However, many of their gains were lost during the economic depression and the bitterly fought strikes of the 1890s. As the economic depression began, many employers' organizations began to fight the unions. The employers wanted to be able to hire workers who were not union members and to pay any wages the workers agreed to, even if they were lower than the level the unions had won. A series of strikes followed from 1890 to 1894.

The Akubra

In the second half of the 19th century, colonial Australians began to forge their own identity, separate from that of the British. One of the symbols of this emerging identity was the Akubra, a felt hat worn by men who lived and worked outdoors. Its broad brim helped shade the wearer from the hot sun. The hat was first made in Tasmania in the 1870s, and later became popular among all Australian men, both country- and city-dwellers alike. The hat gets its name from the Aboriginal word for 'headdress'.

In the 1890 maritime strike, seamen, ships' officers, wharf labourers and shearers all went on strike.

A NEW NATION

By the 1880s, many people began to think that the colonies of Australia would be better off as one country. On 1 January 1901, the Commonwealth of Australia was proclaimed.

By this proclamation, the six separate British colonies in Australia – New South Wales, South Australia, Queensland, Tasmania, Western Australia and Victoria – became one nation under a central authority. The new states' shared national identity was sealed with the foundation of a new capital, Canberra, in 1913. Such an act is known as an act of **federation**.

However, the act of federation did not make Australia completely independent from Britain. Australia was still part of the British empire, and Britain still controlled Australia's relations with other countries.

Most Australians felt a strong loyalty to the British empire and were proud that they belonged to it. Others, however, believed that their country should be independent or even that it should be a republic. These ideas were often expressed in the works of the writer Henry Lawson (1867–1922), who saw the true Australian as a male bush worker who was loyal to his mates and against British snobbishness.

FEDERATION

On 1 January 1901, the six Australian colonies became a single nation. The Northern Territory, which had a tiny non-Aboriginal population of some 3300 people, was ruled directly by the federal government. The British territory of Papua became part of Australia in 1906. New Guinea was given to Australia after World War One.

'White Australia'

During the latter part of the 19th century, thousands of Chinese workers came to the Australian goldfields. They were prepared to work for less than the agreed wage, and many trade unions feared that their own workers would lose their jobs as a result. The unions demanded a policy to keep Australia 'white' by excluding Asian immigration.

Most Australians strongly supported the racist 'White Australia' policy because they feared that non-white migrants would be used as cheap labour. Soon after federation in 1901, the Immigration Restriction Bill was passed to stop non-white migrants from entering Australia. The Pacific Islands Labourers Act was also passed in the same year. It allowed Australia to send back Pacific islanders who had been brought – often by force – to work on the Queensland sugar plantations. Pacific islanders came mostly from the Solomon Islands and the New Hebrides (now called Vanuatu), which at that time were part of the British empire.

In 1932, the Sydney Harbour Bridge was completed and was heralded as a symbol of Australia's new-found modernity.

'A workers' paradise'

In the early 20th century, Australia was often described as a workers' paradise. Skilled workers were well paid even though many other Australians worked very long hours for low pay. In 1904, the Australian parliament set up the Commonwealth Court of Conciliation and Arbitration to solve disputes peacefully between workers and employers. Three years later, the court established the principle of a minimum wage to which a worker should be entitled. Another reform was the introduction in 1912 of compensation for government employees who were injured through their work.

These kinds of reforms were possible in Australia because of the widespread idea that the country should be a fair and just society. However, this attitude did not extend to non-whites. Aborigines and Asian workers were poorly paid and found it difficult to find jobs.

Unions were very powerful. Skilled workers could often not find work unless they belonged to a union. This banner for the Building Trades Union comes from Broken Hill, where the unions were especially powerful. It is protesting against poor-quality housing.

In 1914, the Royal Australian Navy (RAN) sank the German ship *Emden* in the Indian Ocean.

Australian troops were praised for being well trained and brave in battle. These men have signed up to fight for the Second AIF during World War Two. The soldiers wear the distinctive slouch hats that were made by the same company that made the Akubra.

World War One

When Great Britain declared war on Germany on 4 August 1914, Australians rushed to enlist. They believed they should be willing to die for their country and empire and wanted to prove Australia's worth to Britain. As the conflict dragged on, however, it began to divide people more and more. Australia had the only fully voluntary army in the war. When the government tried unsuccessfully to get public support for conscription (drafting) in 1916 and 1917, it divided the Australian people.

Australia recruited an army named the Australian Imperial Force (AIF). It was combined with New Zealand's troops to form the Australian and New Zealand Army Corps (ANZAC). The **Anzacs** fought against Germany's ally, Turkey, on the **Gallipoli** Peninsula, where they aimed to capture the Dardanelles, a narrow strip of water. The British believed that control of the Dardanelles would shorten the war (see pages 72–3). The Anzacs also fought in the Middle East and against German troops in France and Belgium.

The war had a terrible impact on Australia. It had a population of under 5 million, yet as many as 330,000 served overseas. Nearly 65 per cent became casualties, and 60,000 were killed. Hardly a family was unaffected by the fighting, and today almost every town in Australia has a memorial to the war dead.

The Great Depression

The next major challenge for Australia in the 20th century came with the **Great Depression** of the 1930s. This worldwide economic slump affected Australia more than most other countries because Australia was an exporter of primary products such as wool and wheat. When the world depression struck, the prices of these products collapsed, and loans to Australia from overseas countries quickly dried up. In 1932, Australian unemployment reached 30 per cent.

People who lost their jobs had to line up for the dole (unemployment benefit). In most states, the dole was not issued as cash, but as coupons that were exchanged for food. People who could not pay their rent faced the threat of homelessness. Many families had to live in ramshackle towns built from discarded materials on bare ground. Because there had been no armed conflicts in Australia during World War One, for many Australians the Depression was worse than the war.

Australia in World War Two

In September 1939, Australia had barely emerged from the Depression when it was again called upon to fight for the British empire against the Germans. A Second AIF was formed from volunteers to fight overseas. There was also a militia for Australia's home

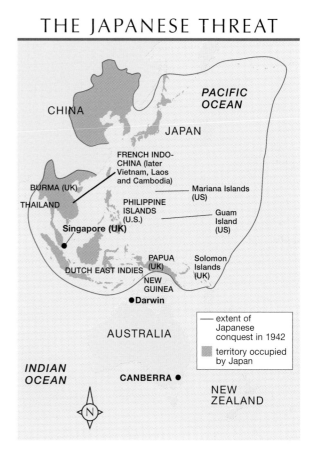

THE JAPANESE THREAT

CHINA

PACIFIC OCEAN

JAPAN

FRENCH INDO-CHINA (later Vietnam, Laos and Cambodia)

BURMA (UK)

THAILAND

Mariana Islands (US)

PHILIPPINE ISLANDS (U.S.)

Guam Island (US)

Singapore (UK)

PAPUA (UK)

Solomon Islands (UK)

DUTCH EAST INDIES

NEW GUINEA

Darwin

AUSTRALIA

INDIAN OCEAN

CANBERRA

NEW ZEALAND

— extent of Japanese conquest in 1942

territory occupied by Japan

N

defence. Three of the four new AIF divisions were sent to the Middle East, where they fought against the Germans and the Italians, who were the Germans' allies.

Japan entered the war when it attacked Malaya and the United States' naval base at Pearl Harbor on 7 December 1941. This widened the war to include Asia and the Pacific and brought the United States in on the Allied side.

Australians thought that Singapore and its British naval base could never fall. By the end of January 1942,

By April 1942, Japanese forces had overrun much of South-East Asia. Many Australians feared that their country would be invaded by the Japanese.

71

Gallipoli: The Anzac legend

SOUTH AUSTRALIANS

COO-EE!

FALL IN!

WE WANT YOU AT THE FRONT

COME AND HELP ENLIST AT ONCE

This poster from South Australia is encouraging young Australian men to enlist to fight in the war. Many men were eager to join at first.

The land attack on the peninsula was carried out mainly by troops from Great Britain and its empire, including the Australia and New Zealand Army Corps, or Anzacs.

On 25 April 1915, the day of the landing on Turkey's Gallipoli Peninsula, the Anzacs had to fight their way up steep cliffs under relentless Turkish gunfire. When night fell, they held only a few kilometres of cliffs and gullies. Some 2300 men died in the landing. Many of them had got no further than the beach where they had landed.

The British had a plan to allow other soldiers to capture the high ridges. As part of this plan, the battles of Lone Pine and the Nek were fought in August. The Anzacs showed great bravery in these battles. Many men died, but the Anzacs gained no advantage over the Turkish enemy.

The campaign lasted until December. The Anzacs made bayonet charges to gain control of the heights since their only hope of victory lay in possessing the cliffs. These charges resulted in enormous losses from Turkish rifle and machine-gunfire.

Eventually, the British decided that victory was not possible and withdrew their troops. When the Anzacs withdrew

In the Gallipoli campaign during World War One, the role of the Anzacs was crucial in an attack on Germany's ally, Turkey. The attack was part of a plan to shorten the war, but it went disastrously wrong from the start.

The main aim of the campaign was to capture the Dardanelles, a narrow strip of water between Turkey's north-western coast and the Gallipoli Peninsula. The British and French thought that by controlling the Dardanelles, they would more easily be able to capture the Turkish capital, Constantinople (now Istanbul).

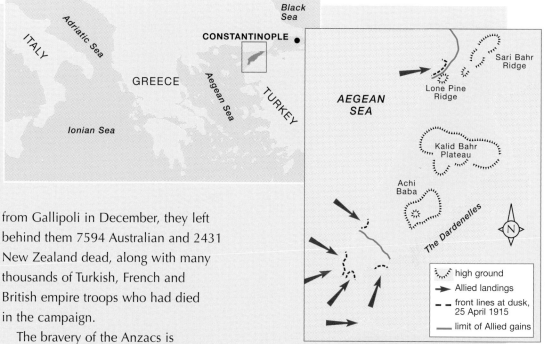

from Gallipoli in December, they left behind them 7594 Australian and 2431 New Zealand dead, along with many thousands of Turkish, French and British empire troops who had died in the campaign.

The bravery of the Anzacs is commemorated throughout Australia every year on 25 April – Anzac Day. Many people consider that the experience of Gallipoli made Australians feel they were one nation for perhaps the first time.

(Above) On 25 April 1915, Allied forces, including Anzac troops, landed on the Gallipoli Peninsula. (Below) These Australian soldiers at Gallipoli are using periscopes to view the enemy territory.

however, the Japanese had taken Malaya and, after savage attacks, the British Command in Singapore surrendered. The defenders of Singapore, including 15,000 Australians, became prisoners of war. By April 1942, Japan had overrun much of South-East Asia, and Darwin had suffered the first of many bombing raids. The war came even closer when, in June 1942, two Japanese midget submarines were sunk in Sydney Harbour. The war ended after the USA dropped two **atomic bombs** on the Japanese cities of Hiroshima and Nagasaki in 1945.

Although evidence now suggests that Japan did not plan to invade Australia, the threat seemed frighteningly real in 1942. Many Australians believed that had it not been for the supremacy of the US Navy in the Pacific, Australia would have fallen to the Japanese.

Robert Menzies

The attitudes of most Australians after World War Two were reflected in the policies of Robert Menzies (1894– 1978), the leader of the Liberal Party and prime minister (head of the federal government) of Australia from 1949 to 1966. Menzies was strongly anti-communist, and his government supported Britain and the USA in wars in Asia, especially in those countries where communist-led movements were trying to seize power, such as in Vietnam.

After World War Two

World War Two had barely ended when the Cold War began. In this time of hostility between the former Soviet Union and the Western nations, communist parties came to power in eastern Europe, North Korea, North Vietnam and China. Fear of **communism** became the main influence on the Western nations' relations with foreign powers. Australia allowed Great Britain to test atomic bombs in the desert regions of Emy Junction and Maralinga.

In order to boost the country's population, postwar governments encouraged **immigration** by offering grants to new settlers. By 1972, more than 4 million people had come to settle. The largest groups of immigrants were still British, but for the first time many people also came from Italy, Greece and other parts of Europe. The Australian government made it clear that no Asian migrants would be allowed to enter Australia, however.

The protest era

The late 1960s and early 1970s were a time of a questioning of past values in Australia. Many people became involved in movements for racial equality, women's and gay rights, environmental issues and world peace. This was part of a wave of change that was sweeping the Western world. One issue united these different movements more than any other: the protest movement against the Vietnam War (see box).

This growing mood of idealism helped the Australian Labor Party win its campaign for the federal elections of December 1972. The party's leader, Gough Whitlam, promised to make Australia a fairer place for all. The government immediately abolished conscription and withdrew Australia's few remaining troops from Vietnam.

Whitlam began a new era of social reform. He introduced free health care and higher education for all and increased funding to the arts. He gave Papua and New Guinea their **independence** and also gave Aboriginal people more rights and began to return their land.

Many people opposed Whitlam's reforms, especially since he had to take out huge overseas loans in order to pay for them. In 1975, opposition parties in Australia used the Senate (see page 79) to block the government's supply of money. Finally, the governor-general, Sir John Kerr, fired Whitlam on 11 November 1975. This landmark event in Australia's history became known as 'the Dismissal'.

In 1975, Australia granted Papua and New Guinea independence as the new nation of Papua New Guinea.

The Vietnam War

The Vietnam War was fought between communist-ruled North Vietnam and US-backed South Vietnam. Australia sent troops in to fight alongside American troops in 1965. Because of the Cold War, the Australian government had introduced the draft in 1964, so many of the Australian soldiers fighting in Vietnam were conscripts. Many Australians supported their country's role in the Vietnam War. Others opposed the war and saw it as interference in another country's affairs. Huge demonstrations took place in Australia. Young men publicly burned their draft cards, and some went to prison rather than accept being drafted. The protests stopped only when Australia's role in the war was officially ended in 1972. In all, some 500 Australians died in Vietnam, and 2300 were injured.

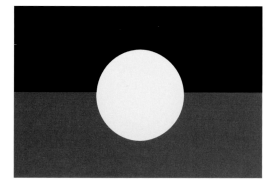

The Aboriginal flag was first flown in 1972. The black area stands for the Aboriginal people, the red is the land and the yellow circle depicts the sun.

Aboriginal rights

In the last few decades, Australian governments have begun to address the wrongs done to indigenous (native) Australians in the past. For much of the 20th century, Aboriginal people who worked on **Outback** cattle stations (farms) were badly paid. Others were forced to live on religious missions or reserves where their lives were controlled by officials.

The Aboriginals Ordinance of 1918 allowed the government to take Aboriginal children from their parents if the father was believed to be white. In such cases, the government decreed that the parents had no rights over their children, who were placed in childcare institutions or foster homes. These children have become known as the 'Stolen Generation'.

After World War Two, the government attempted to assimilate Aborigines into Australian culture. The government told Aborigines where they could live and whom they could marry. Many were forced to live in towns in an attempt to make them adapt to European culture. These moves failed miserably.

Real improvement began in the 1960s. In 1962, all Aboriginal people gained the right to vote in federal elections, although there was still widespread discrimination in rural areas. In the 1960s in the USA, black people and their white supporters had travelled around the country to draw attention

Fred Maynard

One of the greatest campaigners for Aboriginal rights was the Aborigine Fred Maynard (1879–1944). In a letter to the Australian government, he declared Aboriginal rights to equality: 'I wish to make clear on behalf of our people that we wish to accept no condition of inferiority as compared to European people ... That the European people by the acts of war destroyed our more ancient civilisation is freely admitted and that by their vices and diseases our people have been decimated is also patent, but neither of these facts are evidence of superiority. Quite the contrary is the case.'

to racial discrimination. Inspired by these freedom rides, as they were known, a group of Aboriginal and white students set out for several country towns in 1965. They held protests in front of hotels, swimming pools and other public places that had banned Aboriginal people. These protests won support for change.

In 1966, 200 Aborigines called the Guirindji people began a nine-year strike when they walked off a Northern Territory cattle station. This strike started the campaign for Aboriginal land rights. The Guirindji won their fight in 1975, when the land containing their sacred sites was handed back to them by Prime Minister Whitlam.

In 1967, public pressure forced the government to acknowledge that Aborigines had special needs. Many of them did not finish full-time education, and there was a high proportion of unemployed Aboriginal people relative to their total population. In the late 1960s, the federal government set up the Department of

When Australia celebrated its Bicentennial in 1988 – commemorating 200 years of European settlement – many Aborigines protested. They felt their land had been invaded for 200 years and there was no reason to celebrate.

ABORIGINAL LANDS

Since 1976, Australia's federal government has passed several Aboriginal Land Rights Acts, allowing Aborigines to claim back their ancestral lands and sacred sites. This map shows those areas (shown in green) of Australia where Aboriginal lands are legally recognized.

Arnhem Land

Kunmunya

Karlantijpa

NORTHERN TERRITORY

Yandeyarra

WESTERN AUSTRALIA

QUEENSLAND

Anangu, Pitjantjatjara, Yungkutitjara, and Ngaanatjara

SOUTH AUSTRALIA

Maralinga-Tjautja

NEW SOUTH WALES

ACT

VICTORIA

TASMANIA

Aboriginal Affairs to meet the needs of Aboriginal people.

Since then, there have been more gains for Aboriginal Australians. State governments have passed laws to return some land to its original owners, and the Aboriginal and Torres Strait Islanders Commission has been set up to enable Aboriginal people to run their own affairs. Two important judgements of the High Court of Australia overturned the idea that Australia had belonged to noone before 1788 (see page 62). These judgements have now made it possible for the Aboriginal people to regain more of their traditional lands. Despite these gains, Aboriginal people are still among the most disadvantaged Australians.

THE ADMINISTRATION OF AUSTRALIA

Australia has a federal system of government made up of a central (federal) government and state and territory governments. It is also a **constitutional monarchy** – the British Queen is also Queen of Australia, but she has no real power in Australia's system of government. The

Australian federal government is responsible for matters that affect the whole nation, such as the national economy, immigration and defence. The states and territories are responsible for other matters within their own borders, including health, education, housing and transportation. All Australians aged eighteen or over are required by law to vote in all government elections, and they are fined if they fail to vote.

The Australian parliamentary system is based on that of Britain. The federal Parliament has two houses, the House of Representatives and the Senate. There are 148 members of the House of Representatives, which is divided according to the size of the population in each state. New South Wales has 50 members; the Northern Territory has one. General elections, in which members are elected, have to be held at least every three years.

The Senate acts as a house of review. Once a bill (new law) has been passed in the House of Representatives, the Senate debates and votes on it again. It can reject or

The New Parliament House on Capital Hill in Canberra is the seat of Australia's federal government. It is where the federal Parliament sits. It was opened in 1988 and replaced the Old Parliament House, which had been used for 61 years.

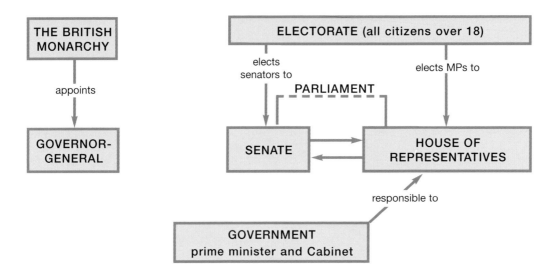

Australia's constitution is a mixture of the US and British systems. Like the United Kingdom, Australia is a monarchy. Like the USA, it is a federation of states.

force changes to proposed new laws. Each state elects twelve senators. The ACT and the Northern Territory each have two senators. State senators serve for six years, territory senators for three years.

The government is formed from the party or **coalition** of parties that has the most members in the House of Representatives. The leader of that party or coalition serves as prime minister and chooses a number of party members to form the Cabinet. The Cabinet members are responsible for each government department.

Except for Queensland, each of the states has its own parliament of two houses. These are known as the Legislative Assembly and the Legislative Council. Queensland abolished its Legislative Council in 1922. State governments are formed by the party or coalition that has the most members in the Legislative Assembly. The leader in state governments is called the premier.

In the USA, the head of federal government and the head of state are the same person – the president. In Australia, the head of state (the governor-general) and the head of federal government (the prime minister) are different people. The official head of government in each state is known as the governor. The governor-general and the state governors represent the Queen in

Australia. In theory, they are appointed by the Queen, but in practice they are chosen by the true heads of government, the prime minister and the premiers. The state governors are ceremonial heads with no real power.

Australia's political parties

The main political parties in Australia are the Australian Labor Party (ALP), the Liberal Party and the National Party. Traditionally, the ALP's strongest support comes from trade unions and working-class people, although it now attracts many middle-class voters. The ALP strongly supports social security benefits for the poor and believes that the government should make adjustments to the economy, such as raising taxes, to achieve equal opportunities and a fairer society.

Both the Liberal Party and the National Party oppose trade unions and support the role of free enterprise – that is, allowing private industry to trade with little government control. By forming a coalition, these two parties have controlled government at federal and state levels more often than the Labor Party.

Australia's prime ministers since World War Two have included:
J. Ben Chifley (1945–9)
Robert G. Menzies (1949–66)
John G. Gorton (1968–71)
Edward Gough Whitlam (1972–5)
J. Malcom Fraser (1975–83)
Robert Hawke (1983–91)
Paul J. Keating (1991–6)
John W. Howard (1996–)

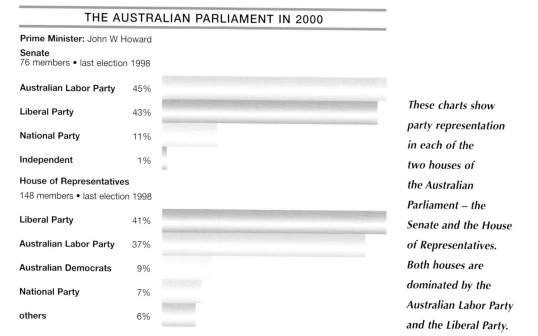

THE AUSTRALIAN PARLIAMENT IN 2000

Prime Minister: John W Howard
Senate
76 members • last election 1998

Australian Labor Party	45%
Liberal Party	43%
National Party	11%
Independent	1%

House of Representatives
148 members • last election 1998

Liberal Party	41%
Australian Labor Party	37%
Australian Democrats	9%
National Party	7%
others	6%

These charts show party representation in each of the two houses of the Australian Parliament – the Senate and the House of Representatives. Both houses are dominated by the Australian Labor Party and the Liberal Party.

The economy

'...agriculture [is] in a yet languishing state; commerce in its early dawn; revenue unknown ... the population depressed by poverty ...'

Lachlan Macquarie (1761–1824), Governor of New South Wales, after his arrival in Sydney in 1810

Much has changed since Governor Macquarie wrote this description of Australia's colonial economy in 1810. For thousands of years, the country's native peoples had maintained a hunting and gathering economy that met all their needs without endangering **natural resources**. The British **colonists**, however, began a completely different kind of economy. Large areas of land were given over to farming and were changed for ever. Wool **exports** and the mining industry both became important in the 19th century. Australian manufacturing, by contrast, was small scale and developed only slowly.

By the mid-1970s, about a quarter of Australia's workforce was in manufacturing, although exports in this sector remained low. Since the 1980s, Australian governments have worked hard to make Australia more competitive in world trade and have encouraged growth industries, such as tourism and wine-growing.

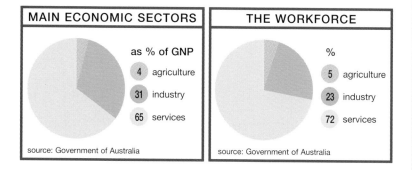

MAIN ECONOMIC SECTORS

as % of GNP

4	agriculture
31	industry
65	services

source: Government of Australia

THE WORKFORCE

%

5	agriculture
23	industry
72	services

source: Government of Australia

This man is shearing a sheep for its wool. Australian wool is among the finest in the world and about 95 per cent of it is exported as raw wool.

MAJOR SECTORS

In the past, wool was an important part of the Australian economy. Most manufactured goods were imported from other countries. Today, the service industries play a much larger part in the total economy.

HOW AUSTRALIA USES ITS LAND

Darwin

Brisbane

Perth

Sydney

Adelaide CANBERRA

Melbourne

Hobart

cropland
forest
pastureland
desert
wetlands

The vast areas of pasture in Australia reflect the fact that cattle and wool are the country's leading farm products.

Agriculture

Vast areas of Australia are used for agriculture, mainly for grazing sheep and cattle, but very few Australians are farmers or farmworkers. Most parts of Australia are too dry for small farms to survive. Huge cattle stations (farms) need few workers: most stock herding, for instance, is done by helicopter. Only one-third of a million Australians work in agriculture.

Most of Australia's crops are grown on the east coast of Queensland and the western slopes and plains of New South Wales and Victoria. The north of Tasmania, the area around Adelaide in South Australia and around Perth in Western Australia are also important crop-growing areas. The main **tropical** coastal crop is sugar cane. The main inland crop is wheat. Australian scientists have developed special kinds of wheat that grow well in the continent's dry climate.

The pastoral, or grazing, industry has been very important in Australia since the 1820s. By the mid-19th century, when Britain was known as the 'workshop of the world', Australia was supplying half of all Britain's raw wool **imports**. However, since the middle of the

20th century, agriculture, including grazing, has become less important for Australia's exports. In 1950, about 80 per cent of Australia's export earnings came from wool, wheat and other farm products. By the 1990s, that figure had fallen to about twenty per cent.

Australian farmers have always faced problems such as droughts, floods and sudden changes in the prices they can get for their produce. In one year, Australian wheat farmers might lose huge proportions of their crops through rain failing to come when it is needed or too much rain falling at the wrong time. In another year, they might have perfect weather conditions and produce far more than usual, only to find that oversupply causes the market price of their crops to fall below what it cost to grow and harvest them.

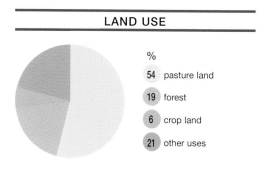

LAND USE

%

54 pasture land

19 forest

6 crop land

21 other uses

source: Government of Australia

(Above) The chart shows the percentage of Australia's usable land given over to various uses. (Below) These sheep are being penned for shearing. Around 75 per cent of Australian sheep are merino, a type first introduced to Australia in 1797.

Wine-growing, a growth industry

One of the most successful industries in Australia in the past two decades has been the production and export of high-quality wines. This is particularly surprising because few Australians drank wine until the late 1960s – Australia was known as a nation of beer drinkers.
For a long time, however, some Australian manufacturers had produced very good wines. German immigrants in South Australia's Barossa Valley were among the industry's pioneers. The first exports of Australian wine occurred in 1822, when Gregory Blaxland shipped wine to London from his estate near Sydney. The wine won a silver medal in a competition held the following year.

Today, Australia is so successful in exporting excellent red and white wines that there are times when growers cannot keep up with the demand. From 1986 to 1996, Australia's wine exports increased 14-fold in volume and 28-fold in value. Some winemakers in France, the home of fine wines, are now copying winemaking methods that were developed in Australia in order to improve their own products.

Today, there are some 50,000 wine-growers working in Australia. Together, they produce about 725,000 tonnes (713,000 tons) of grapes for Australia's more than 900 wineries (winemaking factories). The industry is also a big employer – some 13,000 Australians work as growers and winemakers and in other related jobs.

In recent times, Australian farmers have faced even bigger problems – falling prices and decreasing markets. Since the 1950s, world prices for farm products have been falling almost continuously. This is partly because most other countries protect their farmers from competition with subsidies, so these farmers produce more and more. Australian farm products could be sold much more cheaply than those from Europe, but the **European Union** (EU) does not allow Australia to compete freely with its farmers. So, although Australia's farmers are among the most efficient in the world, their incomes keep falling.

The Australian government has had many plans to help farmers, although some are less successful than others. The Australian Wool Corporation was meant to help sheep farmers sell their wool at a profit. It did this by building up big stocks of wool when prices were low. The idea was that these would be sold when prices were better. However, by 1990 these stockpiles were enormous, and prices kept falling. In this same period, the prices farmers had to pay for things such as fuel and

The interests of Australia's farmers are represented by the National Farmers' Federation (NFF).

Growing olives

Australia's first olive trees were probably planted in Parramatta near Sydney in 1805. The warm, sunny climate of the region was perfect for growing this Mediterranean tree, which is not native to Australia. Soon, there were olive plantations across Victoria and South Australia. Some were even planted in Perth; today, the people of Perth claim that the olive trees growing in front of the city's Parliament House are the oldest in the continent. After World War Two, the arrival of immigrants from traditional olive-growing countries, such as Italy and Greece, encouraged the planting of more olive groves.

However, for much of the 20th century, olive-growing was not economically competitive. Olives and olive oil could be imported into the country far more cheaply than they could be produced at home. Today, the home demand for olive products is far outstripping the supply, and new growing methods and olive varieties are making the industry internationally competitive.

Government agencies closely supervise logging to ensure that the natural forest environment is damaged as little as possible. In the past, many of Australia's native animal species lost their natural habitats because of the destruction of the older forests.

machinery kept rising. The result of all this has been that many of the smaller farmers became so indebted to banks and had so little hope of improving their incomes that they had to abandon farming altogether.

Agriculture is becoming much less important to the overall Australian economy. Economists call the total value of all a country's goods and services produced in a year the **gross national product** (GNP). In 1998, Australia's agriculture, including forestry and fishing, was worth only four per cent of its GNP.

Fishing and forestry

With Australia's long coastline, it is not surprising that fishing is an important industry. One problem, though, is that some of the most valuable species of fish, such as the southern bluefin tuna, have been overfished. To conserve Australia's stocks of fish, the government has had to reduce the numbers of licensed fishing boats and restrict fishing in several areas.

Forestry has also been important to Australia's economy, and large forest areas are harvested and exported. Many of the ancient forests have been cleared, and today only nineteen per cent, or 410,000 square kilometres (158,260 square miles), of the continent's land is forested.

Forestry has been very controversial because many Australians have become concerned about the need to preserve the natural environment. Australians from all walks of life

have protested to save native forests, and there has been a reduction in logging as a result. Some state governments have been forced to pass laws to stop logging in the older forests, especially where it threatens to destroy animal species that depend on these forests.

Minerals and energy

Australia is rich in natural resources and has large reserves of minerals. In the 1950s, Australia's export earnings from mining were just five per cent, but in the 1960s, a new minerals boom began. Mining corporations began mining big deposits of iron ore, bauxite, nickel, uranium, copper, oil and natural gas. By the mid-1970s, the value of minerals production had grown to about half the value of agriculture, and by the 1990s, mining provided more than 40 per cent of Australia's export income – twice as much as agriculture.

This big mining boom began with the industrialization of Japan. As Japan's economy grew stronger, it needed **raw materials** for its industries. During the 1960s, prices in Australia for coal, iron ore and bauxite more than doubled. Like agriculture, mining experiences big swings in profits caused by changes in world markets. Unlike agriculture, though, the mining industry is controlled by huge **multinational companies.**

Mining has proved controversial in Australia because it has sometimes been carried out on land claimed by **Aboriginal people** and because of fears that it might harm the environment. The most divisive issue has been uranium mining (see box). Australia is the

Uranium

As the Earth's fossil-fuel resources dwindle, the importance of nuclear fuels such as uranium increases. Uranium is a silvery white metal that is one of the chemical elements. It forms a relatively rare part of the Earth's crust, but important deposits have been found in Canada, the USA, Zaire and France, as well as in Australia.

Uranium was discovered in 1789 by the German chemist Martin H. Klaproth (1743–1817), who named it after the recently discovered planet Uranus. It was not until the 20th century that its use as a powerful source of energy was discovered.

Australia largely meets its energy needs from its rich coal reserves. It does not use nuclear energy.

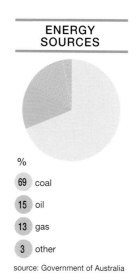

ENERGY SOURCES

%
69 coal
15 oil
13 gas
3 other

source: Government of Australia

This aerial view of a gold mine in Kalgoorlie-Boulder, in Western Australia, shows the craters that have formed where the gold has been mined. Gold was first discovered here in 1893, and today the town is Australia's biggest producer of gold.

world's second-largest uranium exporter, after Canada. Australia does not use nuclear power itself. Many Australians believe that their country should not sell uranium to other countries because of the dangers of nuclear warfare and toxic waste.

In 1997, Australia was the world's biggest producer of bauxite (used to make aluminium), diamonds and zircon, a mineral prized as a gemstone and source of the element zirconium. However, gold and iron ore were Australia's most valuable minerals. Together, they made up 60 per cent of the revenue earned by Australian metallic minerals. The mine at Mount Isa, in Queensland, is the Western world's biggest silver and lead producer.

In 1997, Australia was among the top ten producers of gold, aluminium, nickel, copper and zircon.

Manufacturing and services

Manufacturing and service industries make up by far the biggest part of the Australian economy. By the late 1990s, the service industries had grown to be worth 65 per cent of the Australian economy, while manufacturing, together with mining, was worth 31 per cent.

Since the late 1960s, the proportion of Australians working in manufacturing has been halved, from just under 28 per cent to 14 per cent. This is partly because the Australian government gives manufacturing industries little protection against imported goods. As a result, most clothes and shoes bought in Australia are now made in countries where workers are paid much lower wages than are workers in Australia. Another reason for the change is that machines and robots now do the jobs that used to be done by workers in big industries.

Most Australians now work in the service industries. These industries include such areas as energy supply, building, retail and wholesale trades, transportation, communications, finance, community services, tourism and recreation. One growing service industry that has done

The map below shows where Australia's major industries are situated.

MAJOR INDUSTRIES

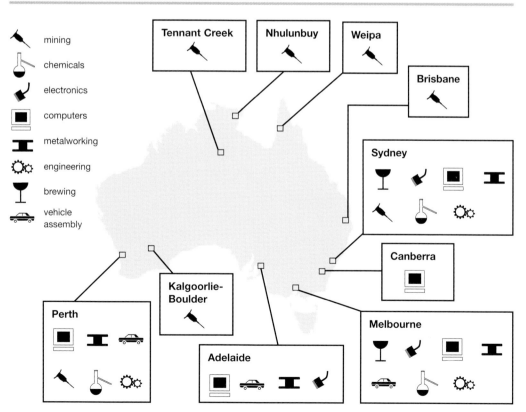

MAIN TRADING PARTNERS

EXPORTS

IMPORTS

%

21.6 Japan

15.5 South-East Asia

11.1 Europe

6.1 USA

45.7 others

%

22.4 Europe

19.9 USA

6.3 Japan

6 South-East Asia

45.4 others

source: Government of Australia

These charts show Australia's main trading partners (above) and its main exports and imports (below).

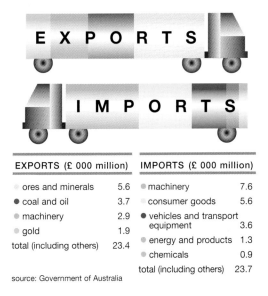

EXPORTS (£ 000 million)

ores and minerals	5.6
coal and oil	3.7
machinery	2.9
gold	1.9
total (including others)	23.4

source: Government of Australia

IMPORTS (£ 000 million)

machinery	7.6
consumer goods	5.6
vehicles and transport equipment	3.6
energy and products	1.3
chemicals	0.9
total (including others)	23.7

much for Australia's trade balance is its world-class education system. Many foreign students, especially from Asia, now study in Australian schools, colleges and universities.

Asia has also become the most important market for tourism in Australia (see chart opposite). Because Australia is a long way from most developed countries in Europe and America, most tourists in Australia are Australians. However, in the 1990s, spending by overseas visitors contributed over six per cent to Australia's GNP. In 2000, the year Sydney hosted the Olympic Games, almost 5 million people from overseas visited Australia, and 5.3 million international visitors arrived in 2001.

The retail and wholesale trades, just two sections of the service industries, now employ more Australians and have a bigger share of the GNP than the whole of Australian manufacturing. This does not mean that Australia's manufacturing, however, has declined. Except for the clothing and footwear industries, it has continued to grow, but not at the same rate as service industries have.

One of the problems that has always faced Australian manufacturers is the small size of the Australian market. In the USA, some manufacturers have a bigger market in one state than exists in the whole of Australia. Many Australians have been disturbed by changes that have seen famous Australian products taken over by overseas companies.

TRANSPORTATION AND COMMUNICATIONS

Australia is a land of vast distances. For example, it takes about a week to travel by car from Sydney, on the east coast, to Perth, in the west. There are many areas where roads are unpaved and can virtually disappear in dust storms or floods.

Cape York Peninsula, in north Queensland, can be reached overland only in a four-wheel-drive vehicle. Travellers on the Birdsville Track in **Outback** New South Wales have to notify the police before they set out so that a search party can be organized if they break down or become lost. Mobile phones are not able to pick up a signal in these remote areas.

MAIN TOURIST ARRIVALS

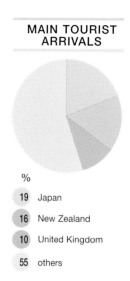

%

19	Japan
16	New Zealand
10	United Kingdom
55	others

The Flying Doctor

Some areas of Australia are so remote that people have to travel hundreds of kilometres to the nearest town. In an emergency, they can call on the Royal Flying Doctor Service. The service was established in 1927. It provides health care in Outback areas by flying doctors and nurses to patients and by transporting patients to a hospital when needed. The service has an extensive system of radio bases and two-way receivers, so that patients can talk about their symptoms to a doctor by radio instead of visiting him or her in person. About 100,000 consultations take place annually, either by radio or via aircraft.

As part of its journey from Sydney to Perth, the Indian Pacific train crosses the vast, arid expanses of the Nullarbor Plain. The train journey can take as long as two or three days.

By contrast, in the densely settled areas, the main roads, motorways and local roads are among the best in the world. Brisbane and Sydney are linked by the Pacific Highway, which follows the coast, and by the New England Highway further inland. Sydney and Melbourne are linked by the excellent Hume Highway and by the slower but more scenic Prince's Highway.

Trains carry passengers and freight in many parts of Australia. Until the second half of the 20th century, travel between states was hampered by different track widths in different states, but this problem has been overcome. Since 1970, Australia has had a transcontinental railway system that uses tracks of the same width.

Air travel has been of great importance in solving Australia's problem of distance. Australian airlines have the best safety records in the world, and all major towns have airports. In remote Outback areas, expert medical care is provided by the Flying Doctor Service (see page 93), in which doctors fly light planes to people in isolated Outback stations and settlements.

In Australia, there has been much political argument in recent years about whether state governments should keep or sell off economic assets such as railways and electricity power plants. There has also been discussion about what the federal government should do with enterprises it traditionally controlled, such as airlines and banks. Generally, the

TRANSPORTATION

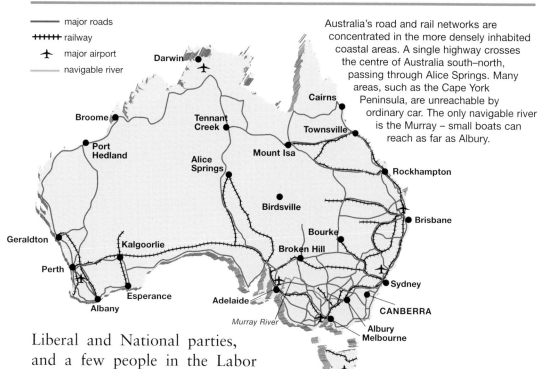

— major roads
++++ railway
✈ major airport
— navigable river

Australia's road and rail networks are concentrated in the more densely inhabited coastal areas. A single highway crosses the centre of Australia south–north, passing through Alice Springs. Many areas, such as the Cape York Peninsula, are unreachable by ordinary car. The only navigable river is the Murray – small boats can reach as far as Albury.

Darwin
Cairns
Broome
Tennant Creek
Townsville
Port Hedland
Alice Springs
Mount Isa
Rockhampton
Birdsville
Brisbane
Bourke
Geraldton
Kalgoorlie
Broken Hill
Perth
Sydney
Esperance
Adelaide
CANBERRA
Albany
Murray River
Albury
Melbourne
Hobart

Liberal and National parties, and a few people in the Labor Party, have favoured selling these enterprises, or **privatizing** them. Other people, particularly in the Labor Party, have argued that these services should remain in government hands because they make money and because only the government will protect the interests of all the people who use these services rather than simply making money.

Australia's national airline, Qantas, is now privately owned, as is the Commonwealth Bank. Just under half of Telstra, Australia's main telecommunications carrier, is also now privately owned.

Travelling by camel

In the 19th century, camels were introduced to Australia as a way of carrying supplies to the continent's most remote settlements. The camels were able to survive the harsh deserts of the Outback and were sturdy pack animals. Caravans of camels often consisted of some 40 animals, each of which could carry around 500 kg (1100 lb) of goods or equipment. Even in 1912, camels were used as water carriers for the Trans-Australian railway. Camels were also useful for exploration – in 1860, 24 camels were brought from India to help with the ill-fated Burke and Wills expedition to the far north of the country (see page 61).

Arts and living

'Australia's postwar immigration policy ... has made Australia a culturally richer ... and much more interesting place to live.'

Former Australian Prime Minister Paul Keating, 1996

Advertising for Australian tourism has encouraged Europeans and Americans to see Australian culture as something represented by the actor Paul Hogan, beer and barbecues – images that tell little of Australia's rich artistic life. The arts of modern Australia draw on many traditions in a land of more than 140 cultural groups. Australia's diversity has influenced its music, films, theatre, dance, painting, sculpture and literature.

Because Australia is such a **multicultural** society, it is not always easy to say what is typically Australian. The uniquely Australian **Aboriginal** culture, long ignored and suppressed, is now experiencing an exciting revival. Works of Aboriginal artists are recognized and highly regarded, both in Australia and around the world. This change has come about in the last 30 years and is part of a wider rebirth of the arts. The cultures of European and Asian migrants have had an increasing influence on Australian life.

Until the 1960s, Australians generally thought that their country had little to contribute to the arts. Although distinctive Australian styles of painting and literature had developed by the late 19th century, Australians tended to regard their own culture as second-rate. The country was referred to by its own people as a 'cultural desert'. So much has changed since then that Australian creative talent is now recognized worldwide.

Surfing is a popular sport in the coastal towns and cities of Australia.
The country's surf beaches are among the best in the world.

FACT FILE

● Until 1788, and the arrival of the British, the cultures of the Aboriginal and Torres Strait Islander peoples had flourished for tens of thousands of years.

● After 1788, settlers tried to turn Australia into another Britain. They brought many British traditions with them, but they never succeeded in making Australian culture quite the same as the British one.

● Since the mid-20th century, Australia has increasingly been influenced by US popular culture, including music, Hollywood films, television (especially soaps) and advertising.

This Aboriginal man from Arnhem Land, in the Northern Territory, is using bark on which to paint (see box). In the past, painters used to add birds' egg yolks, plant resins or wax to the colours to bind them together. Today, Aboriginal painters use wood glue as a binding agent.

Bark painting

Aboriginal people in Arnhem Land, in the Northern Territory, use bark from the stringybark tree on which to paint. They take the bark from the tree in the wet season, when the bark is flexible and moist. Then they dry it and flatten it, ready for painting.

The main colours they use are red and yellow from ochre, white from kaolin and black from charcoal. The paintings are often done in a cross-hatching style and depict Dreaming stories.

THE ARTS

Australian artists, filmmakers and writers have won considerable acclaim, both at home and abroad, and Australian influence in the arts continues to grow. Ordinary Australians are recognizing that their country has much to offer in the arts.

Painting: dots, X-rays and Ned Kelly

The oldest Australian paintings are the work of the Aboriginal and Torres Strait Islander peoples. Although many native artists now use modern materials, they work in a style that was developed tens of thousands of years ago.

Probably their most familiar pictures are 'dot paintings'. Thousands of different coloured dots are used to represent stories from the **Dreaming**. Another traditional style of Aboriginal art can be seen in the 'X-ray' views of people and animals in Arnhem Land, in the Northern Territory (see page 55). In these paintings, the artists depict creatures' bones and internal organs.

Many Aboriginal paintings can still be seen on walls in canyons and caves at, for example, the sites at Ubirr and Nourlangie in Kakadu National Park. The locations of other sites are kept secret by their Aboriginal owners. This is not only because of the danger that the art may become damaged, but also because some sites are sacred to the Aborigines.

The first distinctively Australian art movement among the British **colonists** developed in the 1880s. It was called the Heidelberg school because the artists had a camp at Heidelberg, near Melbourne. This movement was strongly influenced by the Impressionist painters in France. The leading artists of the school were Tom Roberts (1856–1931), Frederick McCubbin (1855–1917), Arthur Streeton (1867–1943), Charles Conder (1868–1909) and Jane Sutherland (1855–1928). They painted outdoors, not in studios, and aimed to capture the changing light, colour and atmosphere of the Australian landscape.

After World War Two, there were several artists who produced work that was so powerful that it became familiar to most ordinary Australians. Russell Drysdale (1912–81) painted rural Australia in all its starkness. Solitary individuals were set in the dramatic, haunting

Albert Namatjira

In the mid-20th century, one of the best-known Australian artists was Albert Namatjira (1902–59), an Aboriginal painter of the Aranda people of Central Australia. Namatjira's paintings of the arid **Outback** quickly became very popular. Although the paintings depict European-style landscapes, Namatjira used warm colours to capture the moods of Central Australia and to convey what Aboriginal people call the 'spirit of the place'.

Namatjira was successful and was able to support many people from his tribe. In 1957, he became the first Aborigine to be granted Australian citizenship (in 1967, all Aborigines were made citizens). Namatjira and his art did much to change white Australians' rather negative view of Aborigines at the time.

(see page 65)

In this painting entitled Bailing Up, *19th-century artist Tom Roberts shows a typical scene of the Australian countryside – bush workers loading produce onto a stagecoach, perhaps ready to take to Melbourne.*

landscapes of the desert. In Drysdale's *The Drover's Wife*, a woman stands like a statue in a dry, bleak and lonely landscape.

In the same period, Sir Sidney Nolan (1917–92) became one of Australia's most popular painters. His paintings explore Australian myths and legends. In 1946–7 he painted his world-famous Glenrowan series about the life and death of Australia's most famous **bushranger**, Ned Kelly (see page 65). Nolan was a sixth-generation Irish-Australian, and his grandfather was a police trooper who had pursued Kelly. Nolan visited Glenrowan, the site of the gang's last stand, before painting the series. Perhaps most famous of the 27 paintings in the series is *Death of Constable Scanlon*. Nolan returned to the Kelly theme again and again.

Stories from the bush and the city

Writers have taken inspiration from Australia's landscape and people since at least the 1880s, when a Sydney newspaper, the *Bulletin*, began to publish the poems of A. B. 'Banjo' Paterson (1864–1941; see page 8) and the short stories and poems of Henry Lawson (1867–1922). Paterson wrote ballads about the **bush** and its people; his most famous composition is 'Waltzing Matilda', Australia's unofficial national anthem (see box).

Lawson was more concerned with social and political issues than Paterson. His short stories tell of the hardships, struggles and loneliness of bush life. Nevil Shute's *A Town Like Alice* (1950) is set in the Australian Outback and was one of the earliest major novels to deal with this subject.

Today's Australian writers identify with the cities and suburbs at least as much as the bush. Among the best-known of modern Australian writers are the novelists Peter Carey (born 1943), Helen Garner (born 1942), the Nobel prize-winner Patrick White (1912–90) and David

In 1973, novelist Patrick White became Australia's first winner of the Nobel Prize for Literature.

'Waltzing Matilda'

'Banjo' Paterson wrote this famous ballad in 1895. It tells the tale of a swagman (drifter) who steals a jumbuck (sheep) and, to avoid being arrested, drowns himself in a billabong (pool). It was once thought of as a meaningless song, but the possibility of a more political theme to the song has recently emerged.

The 1890s were turbulent times in Queensland. Widespread sheepshearers' strikes, unemployment and economic hardship rocked the state, against a background of national calls for Australian federation. Visiting Winton in Outback Queensland, Paterson heard stories about a violent shearers' strike in 1894 at Dagworth Station (a sheep farm), during which shearers burned down several woolsheds. A bounty was placed on the head of the rebels' leader, Samuel Hofmeister, who drowned himself in a billabong to escape the law.

It is difficult to prove a direct link between these events and 'Waltzing Matilda'. However, the song's rebellious tone made it an ideal anthem for rebel shearers at the time. It has appealed to Australians in general ever since.

The didgeridoo is a musical instrument native to Australia. Traditionally, it was played by Aborigines in ceremonies, and was made from a eucalyptus branch that had been hollowed out by termites. In order to play it properly, the player must master the technique of 'circular breathing'. This involves blowing into the instrument while also taking in air through the nostrils.

Malouf (born 1934), who won the Commonwealth Prize for fiction with his novel *The Great World* (1991). Tim Winton (born 1960) is regarded by many as one of the best writers in Australia today. His novels include *Cloudstreet* (1991) and *The Riders* (1994), both of which feature superb descriptions of coastal Western Australia. Australian poet Les Murray (born 1938) is acclaimed worldwide.

Since the 1970s, there has also been a rebirth of Australian theatre. This is largely because a few adventurous theatre companies, mainly in Sydney and Melbourne, gave young playwrights, including David Williamson (born 1942) and Alex Buzo (born 1944), the chance to have their work performed.

Didgeridoos and fiddles

Australian folk music takes inspiration from English, Irish and Scottish influences. To this day, country – or bush – bands use instruments such as fiddles, tin whistles and banjos to play fast-paced dancing music.

By the 1970s, composers such as Peter Sculthorpe (born 1929) looked to Australia's landscapes for inspiration. So did many rock and roll artists, even though most rock music tended to copy the styles coming from the USA and Britain. In the 1980s, bands such as Australian Crawl, the Dingoes, Cold Chisel, Goanna and Midnight Oil composed and performed songs on wholly Australian themes, while INXS attained success on a global scale.

Over the past decade, Aboriginal performers have also become more widely appreciated. The song 'Treaty', by Aboriginal band Yothu Yindi, concerns broken land agreements and has done much to bring attention to Aboriginal land claims. The band's lead singer, Mandawuy Yunupingu, was declared Australian of the Year in 1993.

At the 'flicks'

In the first decades of the 20th century, Australian filmmakers were among the pioneers of motion-picture making. Charles Tait's *The Story of the Kelly Gang*, made in 1906, was one of the world's first feature films. In the 1920s, going to the 'flicks', as films were called, became one of the most popular pastimes in Australia. After World War Two, the Australian film industry collapsed, however, as people flocked to see the Hollywood films.

All this changed dramatically in the late 1960s, when state and federal governments set up organizations to promote filmmaking in Australia. Gough Whitlam's Labour government introduced generous grants for filmmakers in the early 1970s. The creation of the Australian Film School in 1973 further encouraged Australian film talent. The 'new wave' of Australian movies included both 'ocker' films and quality films. 'Ocker' films were comedies featuring rough-and-ready heroes. The first was *The Adventures of Barry McKenzie* (1972). This form of Australian film continued into the 1990s; the most successful examples of recent times are Paul Hogan's *Crocodile Dundee* movies of the 1980s and 1990s.

Peter Weir's mysterious *Picnic at Hanging Rock* (1975) was one of the finest films of the 1970s. Gillian Armstrong's *My Brilliant Career* (1979), the story of a

Yothu Yindi

The Aboriginal band Yothu Yindi has played throughout the world. Many of its songs are about the Aboriginal people's bond with the land and their respect for nature.

'Yothu Yindi' means 'mother and child'. The band uses both Aboriginal instruments, such as the didgeridoo, and electric instruments, such as the guitar. The band's music is a mix of rock and Aboriginal music that has proved popular with all kinds of Australians.

Historians consider the Australian film *Soldiers of the Cross* as the world's first feature film. It was screened at Melbourne Town Hall in 1902.

Henry Lawson, the 'people's poet'

The poet and short-story writer Henry Lawson thought that Australia should break its ties with Britain and become a republic. In 1887, he wrote 'A Song of the Republic', his first published poem. It called upon Australians to rise up and free their country from the ways of the old, colonial world. The first two verses are as follows:

Sons of the South, awake! arise!
Sons of the South, and do.
Banish from under your bonny
*   skies*
Those old-world errors and
*   wrongs and lies,*
Making a hell in a Paradise
That belongs to your sons
*   and you.*

Sons of the South, make choice
*   between*
(Sons of the South, choose
*   true),*
The Land of Morn and the
*   Land of E'en,*
The Old Dead Tree and the
*   Young Tree Green,*
The Land that belongs to the
*   lord and the Queen*
And the Land that belongs
*   to you.*

young woman's struggle for independence, was another highpoint, as was Weir's *Gallipoli* (1981), a film about the **Gallipoli** campaign in World War One.

The result of this growth has been a distinctive Australian filmmaking that is respected throughout the world. Today, Australian filmmakers, technicians and actors are increasingly in demand overseas, Hollywood included. Feature films such as *Strictly Ballroom* (1991), *The Adventures of Priscilla, Queen of the Desert* (1994) and *Shine* (1996) have become worldwide successes. There has also been an increase in the number of women producers and directors over recent years.

Making buildings Australian

Most of the earliest buildings in Australia date from the gold-rush era of the 1850s. The great wealth that was created went towards constructing grand buildings in the Victorian style. Most cities and major towns still have some buildings of this type.

At the turn of the 19th century, a new style developed, called 'Federation'. Built between about 1890 and 1920, Federation houses usually have red brick walls and an orange-tiled roof.

Verandas are a common feature on most Australian houses. Not only are they a pleasant and shady place to sit on a hot summer's day, but also they keep the rooms inside dark and cool. The 'Queenslander' is a distinctive style of house, found only in the state of Queensland. Houses are raised on stilts to allow cooling breezes to ventilate the rooms inside.

The Sydney Opera House

Australia has few great works of architecture. Some of the grand buildings of the Victorian era survived the 1950s and 1960s, when much of Australia's architectural heritage was demolished to make way for concrete and glass skyscrapers. In the 1950s, however, the New South Wales government of the time gave the go-ahead for the Sydney Opera House, one of the most daringly original buildings in the world.

Nearly half of all overseas visitors visit this masterpiece, which stands on Bennelong Point, surrounded on three sides by the harbour. It is divided into two sections, and its white-tiled sail-shaped roofs soar 67 m (220 ft) into the air.

When the NSW government launched a competition for the design of an opera house in 1957, a Danish architect, Jøern Utzon, submitted a daring idea for a building with a roof of 'sails'. Construction began in 1959, but its cost kept increasing and it became the butt of numerous jokes in Australia. When Utzon was told to cut costs by working with the government's own architects, he left the project in disgust. The building, which was meant to cost A$7 (£3) million and take five years to build, cost A$102 (£44) million and took fourteen years to build. Regarded as a 'white elephant' in the 1960s, the Opera House is now one of Sydney's most famous symbols.

Paddington, a suburb of Sydney, is known for its attractive terrace houses dating from the Victorian era. The balconies are often decorated with ornate wrought iron, and the roofs are made of corrugated tin, such as the ones shown here.

EVERYDAY LIFE

In 1967, the historian Russell Ward said: 'Where Americans tend to admire the man who fights his way to the top ... Australians tend to admire rather the "battler" – the common man who battles on, is loyal to his mates, but never achieves success except by chance and then he should have the grace to be a little embarrassed by it.' In Australia's multicultural and changing society, it is much harder than it was 30 or more years ago to describe typically Australian characteristics. Yet some of the attitudes of Australians noted by Russell Ward are still true of many Australians today – a disrespect for authority, a dislike of snobbishness, an easygoing approach to life, loyalty to friends and a belief in a 'fair go' for all. In a variety of ways, these characteristics influence the everyday lives of Australia's people.

Australia has been accused of being racist. Although true in the past, now people from all over the world are included easily in its society with little conflict.

Food and drink

Until the 1960s, Australian food ranked among the most unimaginative in the Western world. Families sat down to evening meals of lamb chops or cutlets, usually overcooked and served with boiled beans or peas, carrots and mashed potatoes. The national drinks were hot tea and cold beer. For variety, a family might have Chinese take-away, but even these dishes were less exotic than real Chinese foods. About the only uniquely Australian food was Vegemite, a sticky spread of vegetable extracts applied to buttered bread or toast.

The wave of **immigration** in the 1950s and 1960s brought Greeks, Yugoslavs and Italians to Australia, along with other nationalities. A spirit of multiculturalism began to grow, which in turn brought about a food revolution. Today, fresh meat, fruit and vegetables can be bought quite cheaply in Australia, and Australians

Australia's vineyards (shown in green) are situated mostly in South Australia, Victoria and New South Wales, where the sunny, temperate weather is good for growing grapes. Increasingly, however, good wines are being produced in Western Australia, Tasmania and Queensland.

Australia's vineyards

Australia's vineyards are dotted around south-east and south-west Australia. The most important areas for wine production, however, are the Barossa and Hunter valleys.

The Barossa Valley, about 50 km (30 mi) north-east of Adelaide in South Australia, is the largest producer of quality wines in Australia. The variation of soil and climate in the area means that a wide range of wines can be made. Today, there are nearly fifty wineries, ranging from small-scale specialists to large **multinational** corporations.

The Hunter Valley is located about 200 km (125 mi) north-west of Sydney in New South Wales. There have been vineyards in the Hunter Valley for more than 150 years. Today, there are some fifty vineyards in the area. The varieties Chardonnay and Semillon are the region's best-known white wines, while Pinot Noir and Shiraz are probably the most familiar red wines.

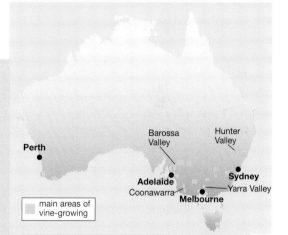

main areas of vine-growing

combine them with exotic ingredients to cook dishes originating from South-East Asia, China, Italy and Greece, among other countries. Over the past decade, local and 'bush' foods have also become popular. Typical bush dishes include emu pâté and braised kangaroo-tail samosas. Barbecues, or 'barbies', are a great Australian tradition. Every weekend when the weather permits, friends and family gather together to eat, drink and socialize outdoors.

Beer remains a popular drink in Australia, although fewer people drink it than ten years ago. Wines come in many varieties. The cellar pack – a wine container that provides wines for everyday drinking – is an Australian invention. Wine has become one of Australia's fastest-growing **exports** (see page 107).

Thanks to the influence of Australia's immigrants, the country's shops and markets now offer a wide range of delicious produce from all over the world. This stand is in Melbourne's famous Queen Victoria Market.

Anzac biscuits

Anzac biscuits are traditionally made on Anzac Day, which is held every year on 25 April. It commemorates all the Australian people who served in wars.

You will need:
110 g (4 oz) plain flour, pinch of salt, 50 g (2 oz) butter, a little cold water

Directions:
Sift the flour and salt into a large mixing bowl. Cut the butter into small cubes and add to the flour. Then gently rub the flour and butter together between your fingers until the mixture is crumbly. Add a little cold water and mix until you have a smooth ball of dough. Wrap it in foil or plastic, and leave it in the refrigerator for 20–30 minutes. Roll the pastry out to a thickness of about 1 cm (1/2 in), and use a cutter or a small glass to cut it into small rounds. Bake the pastry rounds in a preheated oven at 180 °C (350 °F) for 10 minutes until golden brown.

'Aussie Rules'

Frank Hardy, an Australian writer, once commented that Australia was the only country in the world where people knew more about the jockeys than about their writers and artists. Many Australian men still read the sports news in their newspapers before the daily news. Not surprisingly, with so much interest, Australia is one of the world's leading sporting nations.

Australians play four types, or codes, of football: rugby league, rugby union, Australian Rules and soccer. Usually, when Australians refer to 'football', they mean rugby or Australian Rules. The football season runs from March to September (the Australian winter).

Rugby league is the major football code in New South Wales and Queensland. The Australian 'Kangaroos' are frequently world champions in rugby league, and the Australian 'Wallabies' often hold the world championship in rugby union. In Victoria, South Australia and Western Australia, Australian Rules, or 'Aussie Rules' as it is popularly called, is almost a religion; the game is

Australian Rules is a unique form of football that is played only in Australia. Two teams of eighteen players play on an oval field with an oval ball. It is a fast, tough and athletic game.

played only in Australia. Originally developed to keep cricketers fit during winter, the game is a combination of rugby and Gaelic football with a few other local rules thrown in. The first reported game was held in Melbourne in August 1858, and that city is the world centre for Australian Rules. The game of Australian Rules is just as tough and fast as rugby league, with players wearing little body protection.

The game of football as it is known in Europe is called soccer in Australia. Australian children play the game, but the country has struggled at the international level. This is partly because the major football teams in Australia are based on ethnic community clubs founded by European immigrants. This has narrowed support for the National Soccer League teams, reducing the game's attractiveness to young athletes. The Socceroos are the Australian international team.

The story of the Ashes

In 1882, a touring Australian cricket team soundly defeated the English team at the Oval Cricket Ground in London. This marked the first time an English cricket team had been defeated on English soil. In response, the London *Sporting Times* produced the following mock obituary:

In Affectionate Remembrance
of
English Cricket,
Which Died at the Oval
on
29th August, 1882,
Deeply lamented by a large circle of sorrowing
friends and acquaintances.
R.I.P.

NB – The body will be cremated and the ashes taken to Australia.

When England toured Australia in 1882–3, the team captain was presented with an urn containing some ashes. These ashes were the remains of the bails that were burnt after the match. Bails are the pieces of wood that the bowler tries to knock off the stumps during a game of cricket. The English and Australian teams compete every two years for this tiny trophy, although the urn itself never leaves Lord's Cricket Ground in London.

Australians are also world leaders in men's and women's cricket. The country has produced some fine international cricketers, including Richie Benaud (born 1930), Jeff Thomson (born 1950), Shane Warne (born 1969) and the Waugh twins, Mark and Steve (born 1965). The battle with England for the Ashes (see box) remains the most eagerly fought international cricketing competition. Cricket is also one of the most popular sports played by ordinary Australians.

Australian tennis players are among the top-ranking players in the world, including Pat Rafter (born 1972), Mark Philippoussis (born 1976), Rennae Stubbs (born 1971), Todd Woodbridge (born 1971) and Lleyton Hewitt (born 1981). Golf, hockey, netball, surfing and swimming are also popular sports in Australia.

Among Australia's great sporting legends, three names stand out. Les Darcy (1895–1917) was a middleweight boxing champion who won 46 out of 50 recorded fights. Cricketer Sir Donald Bradman (1908–2001) remains one of the greatest batsmen of all time. He scored many hundreds of runs against Australia's great cricketing rival, England. Phar Lap, the legendary racehorse, won 19 of his 21 races, including the 1930 Melbourne Cup. Phar Lap was later taken to the USA.

The Melbourne Cricket Ground (MCG) is the biggest cricket ground in the world. The stadium has space for about 100,000 spectators.

Religion

Most Australians are officially Christian, with the largest groups being the Roman Catholic, Anglican and Unitarian churches. However, recent studies indicate that most Australians attend churches only for christenings, weddings and funerals, and religion does not play a great part in their lives.

Almost every religion has some followers in Australia, and there are now large numbers of Muslims and Buddhists among the population. At the end of the 1990s, the construction of the largest Buddhist temple in the Southern Hemisphere was completed near Wollongong in New South Wales.

Education for all

Australians consider education to be very important. Equal educational opportunity is considered to be the basic right of all Australians. Each state and mainland territory administers its own school system. The character of these systems was established in the 1880s on the principle that schooling should be free, compulsory and secular (free from the control or influence of any one church). There is also an extensive system of private

Australian English

Except for recent immigrants, most Australians speak English with an Australian accent. The accent varies little throughout the country, but it is often stronger in the bush than in the city and stronger in working-class parts of the cities than in middle-class suburbs. In a very strong Australian accent, 'pie' sounds like 'poy'.

Most people outside Australia do not have trouble understanding the Australian accent, but they do find many everyday expressions, or colloquialisms, a bit puzzling. Here are just a few Australian colloquialisms. Some of these are dying out, but they are understood even by those Australians who do not use them.

arvo, afternoon
blue, a mistake, a fight or
   a person with red hair
bonzer, excellent
chook, a chicken
Buckley's chance, no chance
   at all
chuck in, give up
chuck a fit, get angry
chuck a U-ee, make a U-turn
cocky, a farmer
crook, ill or sick

drongo, a fool
earbash, talk non-stop
fair dinkum, genuine
fair go!, be reasonable!
garbo, a rubbish collector
g'day, hello
hooroo, goodbye
lair, a show-off
milko, a milkman
not the full quid, a bit stupid
sheila, a woman
tucker, food

schools in Australia, most of which are run by religious groups. Since the 1960s, these schools have also been assisted by funds from state and federal governments. The largest private system is the parish school system of the Roman Catholic Church.

All Australian children must attend school until the age of fifteen or sixteen, depending on the state in which they live. High-school qualifications have become more important in getting a job, which means that most students stay at school until age seventeen or eighteen.

The main higher education systems are the state-run technical colleges and the universities. The most democratic educational reform of the 20th century took place in the early 1970s, when the federal Labour government provided massive funding increases for universities and abolished university fees. Formerly, only the brightest working-class students – those who won scholarships – could afford to go to university. In the late 1980s, fees for higher education were reintroduced, although students can choose to pay the fees when they have graduated and are earning a salary. However, Australian universities are struggling to maintain equal education opportunities under these conditions.

Health and social security

Australia has an extensive system of social security that provides benefits for the elderly, poor, sick and unemployed. It is based on the belief that everyone who is unable to earn a living – either through age, illness, disability or unwanted unemployment – is entitled to a basic income. The federal government provides benefits to all Australians in need. Australia has a system of free care in public hospitals and government-subsidized medical care through private doctors.

These reforms were almost entirely carried out under Labour governments. However, they are so consistent with the Australian idea of a 'fair go' that few other governments have dared to tamper with them.

EDUCATIONAL ATTENDANCE

college and university	29%
secondary school	99%
primary school	100%

The chart above shows the percentage of young people who attend education at each level.

Australia's health-care programme is called Medicare.

National holidays

1 January	New Year's Day
26 January	Australia Day
March/April	Good Friday and Easter Monday
25 April	Anzac Day
14 June	Queen's Birthday
25 December	Christmas Day
26 December	Boxing Day

National holidays and festivals

Besides the national holidays (see box), each of the states and even some cities have local holidays. For example, the city of Melbourne has a public holiday for the Melbourne Cup, the horse race with the biggest purse in Australia. It is held on the first Tuesday in November, and most people in Australia will stop to watch the race on television or listen to it on the radio.

Australia has many festivals that bring together artists, performers and audiences from around the country and the world. Among the most famous are the Adelaide Festival of the Arts and the Festival of Sydney, but even small towns have major festivals. The Tamworth Country Music Festival is the Australian country music event of the year. Folk, blues, jazz and other kinds of music all have annual festivals, too.

The most unusual of all Australia's festival events is the Sydney Gay and Lesbian Mardi Gras, held in February. This colourful street parade met with some opposition when it was first staged in 1978. Today, however, the Mardi Gras has become an international event. Around 700,000 people turn up to watch it, including many Australians with their young families.

The most patriotic Australian national event is Anzac Day on 25 April. It is neither a festival nor a celebration. It begins at dawn with religious services throughout the country. These are followed by a march, in every city

Australian homes are usually well equipped. In an often warm and dry climate, swimming pools are a luxury that many Australians aspire to.

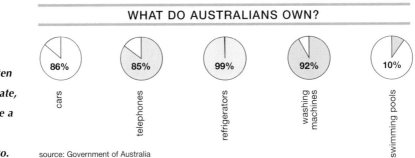

WHAT DO AUSTRALIANS OWN?

86% cars

85% telephones

99% refrigerators

92% washing machines

10% swimming pools

source: Government of Australia

114

and country town, of men and women who served the country in times of war, not just in World War One. It is such a uniquely Australian commemoration that many Australians believe Anzac Day should be Australia's national day.

Newspapers, television and radio

There are far fewer newspapers in Australia now than there were half a century ago, and their ownership is in fewer hands. Indeed, a major cause for concern about the press is that just a few big proprietors now own almost all the major daily papers.

Television is also largely controlled by a few major proprietors. However, in addition to the three commercial stations, Australians have the Australian Broadcasting Corporation (ABC) station and a Special Broadcasting Services (SBS) station. The ABC is wholly government funded, and SBS is partly government funded.

While the commercial stations show mainly American dramas and Australian and American soap operas, most high-quality programmes are provided by the ABC and SBS. These stations provide by far the best news and current affairs programmes. SBS broadcasts films and other shows from all over the world. Although the ABC is fully government funded, it is fiercely independent. It is often far more critical of government policies than its commercial rivals.

Radio is more democratically controlled than television. Besides the commercial stations, the ABC and SBS, there is a huge range of stations operated by community broadcasting groups. Triple J, ABC's youth radio station, is foremost in playing new Australian and overseas bands and in discussing issues of youth culture.

Overall freedom of the press and media is firmly entrenched in Australia. Its only threat comes from the undue influence that a few big media owners are able to have on politicians and the hostility some political leaders have shown towards the independence of the ABC.

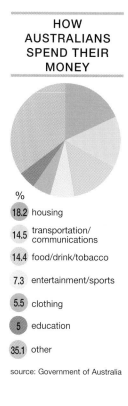

HOW AUSTRALIANS SPEND THEIR MONEY

%
18.2 housing
14.5 transportation/communications
14.4 food/drink/tobacco
7.3 entertainment/sports
5.5 clothing
5 education
35.1 other

source: Government of Australia

This chart shows how the average Australian household spends its income. Australians spend most on maintaining their homes.

The future

'For ordinary Australians ... inequality has increased, jobs have become insecure, working hours are longer.'

Jenny George, President of the Australian Council of Trade Unions, 1997

Australia has experienced enormous changes since it became a nation on the first day of the 20th century. From a backward **colony**, it has grown to become a mature and proud nation with its own strong identity. Provided with abundant **natural resources**, a well-educated workforce and a population rich in cultural traditions, Australia has the potential for growth, prosperity and social harmony.

Many problems and challenges remain, however. At the forefront are questions about racial tolerance and reconciliation, Australia's ties with the British monarchy and economic security and equality.

MONARCHY OR REPUBLIC?

Between 1953 and 1999, public support for Australia breaking its ties with Britain and becoming a republic grew from 23 per cent to 70 per cent. In the last few decades of the 20th century, several changes contributed to increased support for an Australian republic. These changes include Australia's closer defence links with the USA and decreased trade links with Britain, the increase in trade with Asia and the growing proportion of Australians who are from non-British backgrounds.

If Australia were to become a republic, the current federal government favours a system whereby the president (the head of the republic) would be appointed by

A replica of Captain Cook's ship **Endeavour** *floats in Sydney Harbour.*
Australia has come a long way since Cook first landed in Botany Bay.

FACT FILE

- There has been a growing gap between the rich and poor in Australia since the 1980s.

- The United Nations Human Development Report for 1992 put Australia at the bottom of a list of 21 developed countries on equality of income. It found that the top 20% of Australian incomes were nearly 10 times greater than the bottom 20% of incomes.

- The Sydney 2000 Olympic Games helped boost Australia's self-confidence as a successful and dynamic young nation.

Globalization

The term 'globalization' is used to describe the process by which nations become part of a world market. Since the 1980s, Australian governments have believed that free market forces will ensure that average citizens benefit from the economic growth enjoyed by the rich, and that Australia must become more competitive to succeed in the world market.

The most disturbing results of these policies in Australia have been a growing gap between the rich and poor, an unemployment level of about 10% and the creation of an underclass of people who have no hope of participating in Australia's economic activity. Concerned Australians of all political opinions have warned of the danger of creating a two-tiered society.

the prime minister (the head of government). However, some Australians believe that the president should be elected directly by the people. By 2001, support for the British monarchy had fallen so much that the only real barrier to Australia becoming a republic was a division between those who want a president elected by the people and those who want a president appointed by the prime minister. Whatever eventually happens, it seems very likely that, at some stage in the near future, Australia's system of government will change.

RECONCILIATION

Multiculturalism has brought many benefits to Australia. However, in 1996 this issue became a matter of intense public debate when a member of parliament made a speech calling for a halt to Asian immigration and an end to multiculturalism. Significant numbers of Australians, especially in rural areas, expressed support for such views. Most Australians, however, appear to want Australia to remain a society free from discrimination.

Reconciliation between **Aboriginal** and non-Aboriginal peoples is one of the most important issues facing Australia in the 21st century. In 1991, the Council for Reconciliation was established. It aimed for 'A United Australia which respects this land of ours; values the Aboriginal and Torres Strait Islander heritage; and provides justice and equity for all'. At the beginning of the 21st century, the main obstacle to reconciliation is the reluctance shown by the current federal Liberal–National **coalition** government to speed up progress on Aboriginal land rights.

ECONOMIC CHANGES

At the start of the 20th century, most Australians gave their support to building a society based on social security reforms that would protect people from poverty. At the same time, they also wanted wage levels that would ensure decent standards of living for workers. The last years of the 20th century saw high levels of unemployment, increased inequality and government attacks on the role and power of unions.

Many Australians today feel that their country's traditions of egalitarianism and a 'fair go' for all can no longer be taken for granted. The greatest challenge for Australia will be meeting the demands of the future without losing the best of the nation's traditions.

Australia is one of the founder members of the trade group known as the Asia-Pacific Economic Cooperation (APEC). Established in 1989, APEC recognizes the interdependence of the Asia-Pacific, or 'Pacific Rim', countries and promotes open trade between its members. At present, there are 21 members of APEC, shown on the map below.

ASIA-PACIFIC ECONOMIC COOPERATION

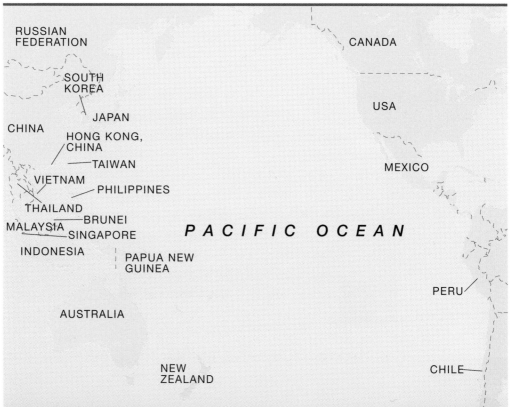

RUSSIAN FEDERATION

CANADA

SOUTH KOREA

JAPAN

CHINA

HONG KONG, CHINA

TAIWAN

VIETNAM

PHILIPPINES

THAILAND

BRUNEI

MALAYSIA SINGAPORE

INDONESIA

PAPUA NEW GUINEA

USA

MEXICO

PACIFIC OCEAN

PERU

AUSTRALIA

NEW ZEALAND

CHILE

Almanac

POLITICAL

country name:
official form: Commonwealth of
    Australia
short form: Australia

nationality:
    noun and adjective: Australian

official language: English

capital city: Canberra

type of government:
    constitutional monarchy

suffrage (voting rights):
    everyone eighteen years and
    over

independence: 1 January 1901

national anthem:
    'Advance Australia Fair'

national holiday:
    26 January (Australia Day)

flag:

GEOGRAPHICAL

location: between the Indian Ocean
    and the South Pacific Ocean;
    latitudes 11° to 44° south and
    longitudes 113° to 154° east

climate: generally arid to semi-arid;
    temperate in the south, tropical
    in the north

total area: 7,692,000 sq km
    (2,970,000 sq mi)
    land: 99%
    water: 1%

coastline: 25,760 km (16,006 mi)

terrain: mostly low plateau with
    deserts

highest point: Mount Kosciusko
    2228 m (7310 ft)

lowest point: Lake Eyre
    −16 m (−52 ft)

land use:
    permanent pasture: 54%
    forests and woodland: 19%
    arable land: 6%
    other: 21%

natural resources: iron ore, bauxite, nickel, uranium, copper, gas, coal, oil

natural hazards: floods, droughts, cyclones, bushfires

POPULATION

population (2002 est.): 19.546,792

population growth rate (2002 est.): 0.96%

birth rate (2002 est.): 12.71 births per 1000 of the population

death rate (2002 est.): 7.25 deaths per 1000 of the population

sex ratio (2002 est.): 99 males per 100 females

total fertility rate (2002 est.): 1.77 children born per woman

infant mortality rate (2002 est.): 4.9 deaths per 1000 live births

life expectancy at birth (2002 est.):
total population: 80 years
male: 77 years
female: 83 years

literacy:
total population: 100%

ECONOMY

currency: Australian dollar (A$); 1 dollar = 100 cents

exchange rate (2001): £1 = A$2.70

gross national product (2001 est.): £290,625 million

gross national product by sectors:
agriculture: 3%
industry: 25%
service: 72%

GNP per capita (2001 est.): £15,000

average annual growth rate (1990–99): 4.1%

average annual inflation rate (1990–2000): 2.2%

unemployment rate (2001): 6.7%

exports (2001 est.): £43,000 million

imports (2001 est.): £43,875 million

foreign aid given: £558.7 million

Human Development Index
(an index scaled from 0 to 100 combining statistics indicating adult literacy, years of schooling, life expectancy and income levels):
92.9 (UK 91.8)

TIMELINE – AUSTRALIA

World history

Australian history

c.50,000 BC

c.40,000 Modern humans – *Homo sapiens sapiens* – emerge

c.40,000 Humans begin to immigrate to Australia from Asia

c.10,000 BC

c.6000 Rice cultivation starts in Asia

c.2500 Ancient Egyptians build the pyramids and Sphinx in Giza

c.15,000 After the end of the Ice Age, the sea rises and Australia becomes an isolated island

c.3000–4000 Aborigines domesticate the dingo

c.AD 1500

1492 Christopher Columbus arrives in North America – Europe begins period of global exploration and colonization

1886–1900 Gold rushes in Canada and South Africa

1842 The British add Hong Kong to their empire

1837 Queen Victoria ascends the throne in Britain

1807 Britain outlaws the slave trade

c.1750 The Industrial Revolution begins

1619 Europeans import the first slaves into the USA

c.1850

1868 End of convict transportation to Australia

1855–90 States achieve self-government

1851–61 Gold rushes contribute to exploration and population and economic growth

1850 British Act of Parliament permits colonies to run their own internal affairs

1836 South Australia is colonized

1829 Western Australia is colonized

c.1800

1788 Sydney is founded as a British convict colony

1770 Captain James Cook claims New South Wales for Britain

c.1700

c.1900

1901 The British queen, Queen Victoria, dies

1910 South Africa becomes independent from Britain

1914–18 World War One

1901 The Commonwealth of Australia is established

1914–18 World War One – over 300,000 Australian volunteers fight in the Middle East and on the Western Front

2000 The West celebrates the Millennium – 2000 years since the birth of Christ

2000 Sydney hosts the Olympic Games

1999 Australians vote to keep the British monarch as their head of state

c.1995

c.1920

1931 Britain establishes the Commonwealth of Nations

1939–45 World War Two

1940 The Battle of Britain

1941 The USA enters the war

1942 The British colony of Singapore falls to Japan

1945 The USA drops an atomic bomb on Hiroshima, Japan

1947 India gains independence from Britain

1927 Seat of federal government is moved to Canberra

1929–39 The Great Depression causes unemployment and poverty

1931 Australia gains its independence

1941 Australia appeals to the USA for military help, marking the end of its exclusive relationship with Britain

1942 Japan begins bombing of Darwin

1997 The British territory of Hong Kong is reunited with China. Tony Blair becomes the British prime minister.

1989 The fall of the Berlin Wall

1975 Governor-General dismisses Prime Minister Whitlam, causing a constitutional crisis

1974 'White Australia' policy is abolished

c.1970

1969 The first human lands on the Moon

1963–75 The Vietnam War

1961 South Africa becomes a republic and leaves the Commonwealth of Nations

1949 Communist regime is founded in China

1967 Aborigines are granted full Australian citizenship

1965–72 Australian troops participate in the Vietnam War

1948–75 'Populate or perish' policy causes huge influx of immigrants from Europe

c.1950

Glossary

Aborigines/Aboriginal peoples Australians whose ancestors were the first peoples to live in Australia

Anzacs (Australian and New Zealand Army Corps) combined Australian and New Zealand army that fought in World War One (1914–18)

atomic bomb extremely powerful bomb that uses the energy released when the nucleus of an atom is split

bush inland region of flat desert and uncleared country

bushranger legendary outlaws who lived in the bush

coalition sharing of government between two or more political parties

coat of arms emblem of a country or family; usually made up of symbolic objects or animals

colonists people who settle in a colony

colony overseas territory settled by another country

communism political system in which goods and land are owned by everyone and in which there is no private property

constitution fundamental principles that underlie the government of a country

constitutional monarchy monarchy that rules according to a constitution

coral craggy marine formation created by living and dead colonies of small marine animals

democratic process that allows the people of a country to govern themselves, usually by voting for a leader or leaders

dialect variation of a language

dingo wild dog

Dreamtime/Dreaming according to Aborigines, the time when the world was created by the spirits

European Union (EU) organization made up of European countries that work together on economic, social and political issues

exports goods sold to one country by another

federation central governing body of a country that has self-governing states

Gallipoli peninsula in Turkey; during World War One, the scene of a famous assault by Anzac and Allied soldiers

Great Barrier Reef coral mass that stretches along the coast of northern Queensland

Great Depression worldwide economic slump in the 1930s

gross national product (GNP) total value of goods and services produced by the people of a country during a period, usually a year

immigration arrival and settlement in a country of people from overseas

imports goods bought by one country from another

independence freedom of a nation or people from the rule of another nation

industrialized nation country where manufacture is often carried out with machinery

marsupials mammals that give birth to underdeveloped young that climb into their mothers' pouches to continue growing

migration movement of individuals or groups from one place to another

monotremes egg-laying mammals found only in Australia

multicultural society where different cultures and races live peacefully together and diversity is celebrated

multinational company company with divisions in more than two countries

natural resources minerals and other natural phenomena that can be harnessed to provide energy or raw materials for manufacture

nomadic lifestyle that involves migration from place to place in search of food or shelter

Outback sparsely populated desert region of Central Australia

premier leader of the party with the majority in a state parliament

privatization transfer of ownership and control of a business or organization to private individuals or companies

protectionism government policy that 'protects' home-produced goods by imposing high import taxes

raw materials naturally occurring substances that can be used to manufacture consumer goods

subtropical climate zone that borders on the tropical and experiences a similar climate

tropical climate zone that lies between the tropics of Capricorn and Cancer

Uluru world's biggest free-standing rock formation, found in Central Australia; Europeans named Uluru Ayers Rock

Bibliography

Major sources used for this book
Esau, Erika and George Boeck, *Blue Guides: Australia.* (WW Norton, 1999)
The Economist, *Pocket World in Figures* (Profile Books, 2002)
Davidson, Graeme, *The Oxford Companion to Australian History* (Oxford University Press, 1998)
Hughes, Robert, *The Fatal Shore: The Epic of Australia's Founding* (Vintage Books, 1986)

General further reading
Clawson, Elmer, *Activities and Investigations in Economics* (Addison-Wesley, 1994)
Martell, Hazel M, *The Kingfisher Book of the Ancient World* (Kingfisher, 1995)
The DK Geography of the World, (Dorling Kindersley, 1996)
The Kingfisher History Encyclopedia (Kingfisher, 1999)
Student Atlas (Dorling Kindersley, 1998)

Taborelli, Giorgio, *Art: A World History* (Dorling Kindersley, 1998)

Further reading about Australia
Arnold, Caroline, *Dinosaurs Down Under: And Other Fossils from Australia* (Clarion Books, 1994)
Darian-Smith, Kate, *People and Places: The Australian Outback and Its People* (Thompson Learning, 1995)
Gutnik, Martin, *Wonders of the World: Great Barrier Reef (*Raintree Steck-Vaughn, 1994)
Nunukul, Oodgeroo, *Dreamtime: Aboriginal Stories* (Lothrop Lee & Shepard, 1994)

A website about Australia
Australian Bureau of Statistics: *www.abs.gov.au*

Index

Page numbers in *italics* refer to pictures or their captions.

Acknowledgements

Cover photo credit
Corbis: Dallas and John Heaton

Photo credits
Art Archive: 62, 100; National Library of Australia 63; Australian Tourist Commission: 11, 38, 42, 109; **Rachel Bean:** 14, 21, 22, 40, 50, 69, 106, 108; **Corbis:** Australian Picture Library 25, 96; Peter Johnson 17; Kit Kittle 93; Wayne Lawler: Ecoscene 88; Matthew McKee: Eye Ubiquitous 77; Charles O'Rear 86; Christine Osborne 48; Paul A. Souders 34, 44, 79; Michael S. Yamashita 82, 85; **Robert Hunt Library:** 70, 73; **Peter Newark's Historical Pictures:** 57, 58, 60, 61, 65, 66, 72; **Tony Stone Images:** Doug Armand 12; Martin Barraud 18; Robert van der Hilst 30; Zigy Kaluzny 105; Gary John Norman 116; Rotman 39; Kevin Schafer 32; Mike Severns 19; Robin Smith 26, 90, 94; Paul Souders 102; Oliver Strewe 27; Darryl Torckler 46; Penny Tweedie 29, 36, 98; Stuart Westmorland 6; **Werner Forman Archive:** Private Collection, Prague 55; Tara Collection, New York 54.